Revolutionary Mothers

Revolutionary Mothers

Women in the Struggle for America's Independence

Carol Berkin

LARGE PRINT

This large print edition published in 2005 by
RB Large Print
A division of Recorded Books
A Haights Cross Communications Company
270 Skipjack Road
Prince Frederick, MD 20678

Published by arrangement with Knopf Subsidiary Rights

Publisher's Cataloging In Publication Data
(Prepared by Donohue Group, Inc.)

Berkin, Carol.
    Revolutionary mothers : women in the struggle for America's independence /
Carol Berkin.

    p. (large print) ; cm.

    Includes bibliographical references.
    ISBN: 1-4193-5013-7

1. Women—United States—Biography. 2. Large type books. 3. United States—
History—Revolution, 1775-1783—Women. 4. United States—History—
Revolution, 1775-1783—Participation, Female. 5. United
States—History—Revolution, 1775-1783—Biography. I. Title.

E276.B47 2005b
973.3/082

Printed in the United States of America

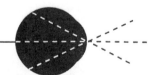

**This Large Print Book carries the
Seal of Approval of N.A.V.H.**

For my brother, Mark Berkin,
and my sister, Sylvia Berkin Rose

CONTENTS

INTRODUCTION

CLIO'S DAUGHTERS, LOST AND FOUND

For many Americans the Revolution is their last great romance with war. We read it as a story of noble generals, brave citizen-soldiers, dashing French noblemen, eloquent statesmen, and freedom-loving wives and daughters. In popular vignettes of the war, there are heroic commanders standing tall in rowboats, and lovely women busily stitching together the new American flag. The events leading to the Revolution seem to move as fast as light, leaping from Plymouth Rock to the Declaration of Independence to Yorktown, as if America's straight trajectory to nationhood was preordained. Although the Revolution is acknowledged to be a "war," it is both a quaint and harmless war, for there is much that is missing in the tales we tell: the violence on and off the battlefield, the families torn apart by political choices, the destruction of homes and crops, the cries of frightened children, the screams of women raped by soldiers, the weariness of a war-torn country, the sickly scent of death and dying in makeshift hospitals, the hunger, dislocation, and for many, both white colonists and Indians, the final exile from their homeland.

In an era of genocidal wars, terrorism, and heated debates over the meaning of patriotism, this romantic view of the American Revolution is especially appealing. But the men and women who lived through it have a very different story to tell, more complex, and, in the end, more relevant to us as their heirs and descendants. As colonists, these Americans were sharply divided on the question of independence. In many areas, the Revolution was a bitter civil war, pitting neighbor against neighbor, rich against poor, and race against race. It was also a brutal home-front war, waged by a largely agricultural society against the most powerful and well-trained military and naval force of the Western world. It was a long war, an eight-year war, begun even before a declaration of independence was signed and continuing, sporadically, after peace was declared. And when it was over, thousands of refugees left their homes, taking with them their skills, their labor, and their knowledge as well as what wealth they could preserve. In its wake it left widows and mourning mothers, disabled veterans, African Americans separated from their families, Indians in danger of losing their lands, a colossal war debt, pockets of economic depression, and a host of political problems that would not be addressed until the constitutional convention of 1787.

The Revolution also left much undone. The eighteenth-century embrace of freedom, liberty, and equality was not yet wide enough to encompass women, men without property, African Americans, or Indians. The limitations the founders of the nation placed upon equality were acts of conformity to the social views of the day as much as deliberate exclusions. For the men who led the country were products of a culture far different from our own, a hierarchical world of deference and obedience. Although they dared to challenge authority for themselves, they did so for specific and compelling political reasons. They did not see their defiance of the king as an invitation to open the floodgates to challenges based on race or gender. Although new ideas about human abilities and capacities, and about the organization of society, had begun to appear, most eighteenth-century Americans grew up in a world of fixed truths about the capacities of men and women, the character of rich and poor, the inherent virtues and shortcomings of white and black. The Revolution disturbed and occasionally reconfigured, but it did not fully dislodge the power of those truths. No sweeping social revolution followed in the wake of the political revolution; indeed, like women and men after many wars, white Americans seemed more eager to return to the life that had been disrupted than to create a new one. Fulfilling the Revolution's promise of equality became the task of the centuries that followed.

It is important to tell the story of the Revolution and its aftermath with the complexity it deserves. But it is also important to tell it as a story of both women and men. Too often the war for independence is portrayed as an exclusively male event, its cast of characters such familiar figures as Commander in Chief George Washington, the "Swamp Fox" Francis Marion, the Virginia orator Patrick Henry, the schoolteacher-turned-spy Nathan Hale, and the midnight rider Paul Revere. Only three women seem to be readily associated with the war for independence: Abigail Adams, who, it is said, requested that her husband and his fellow lawmakers of the new nation "remember the ladies" and let them vote; Betsy Ross, who sewed the first United States flag; and Molly Pitcher, who carried water to the thirsty men defending Fort Monmouth. Alas, in all three cases, historical memory is faulty. Abigail Adams was not an early suffragist, demanding that John and the Congress grant women the right to vote. She was a dutiful, if politically informed wife, asking privately if her husband could do something to reform the horrendous laws of coverture that deprived married women of their property rights. Betsy Ross was not a humble seamstress but a skilled upholsterer, an artisan with a thriving trade, and although she may have sewn a flag, there is little evidence to prove it. Finally, Molly Pitcher simply did not exist. Like Rosie the Riveter of World War II fame, Molly Pitcher was a name given to the many women who carried water to cool down the cannons so that soldiers could reload and fire them again.

The gender amnesia that surrounds the American Revolution did not always exist. During the war, and in the early decades of the new nation, poets, pamphleteers, essayists, novelists, and many public leaders praised women for their participation in the struggle for independence, even as they debated what new demands, if any, the young republic ought to make upon female patriots and what demands these women could make on the new nation. The experiences of this revolutionary generation of women were kept fresh in the minds of later generations by women like Elizabeth Ellet, whose three-volume *Women of the American Revolution*, published in 1848-1850, was based on letters, diaries, and recollections passed down from mother to daughter to granddaughters. Because of Ellet, antebellum women—and men—could thrill to stories of women who led boycotts against British goods, raised funds for the Continental Army, nursed wounded soldiers, spied on the enemy, and wrote propaganda to advance the patriot cause.

But if Ellet's work honored the women of the revolution, it also transformed them, for her biographical sketches are premised on the nineteenth-century belief in woman's inherent moral superiority, her natural piety, her maternal instincts, and her domestic role as the mistress of a haven from the heartless world of early industrializing society. In the romantic prose of her own era, Ellet recast eighteenth-century icons such as Abigail Adams and Martha Washington as models of a gentility and domesticity familiar to her readers. Abigail and Martha might not have recognized themselves—or each other—from the pages of Ellet's books, but they would have been pleased to see that they remained in the public's memory.

Although many of Ellet's subjects were elite women, there were a surprising number of frontier housewives so obscure that their first names are unknown, as well as young farm girls and soldiers' wives. But rich or poor, most of the women who found a place in *Women of the American Revolution* earned mention because of their devotion to husband, children, and parents. As a group, indeed as a gender, they were virtuous, self-sacrificing, unassuming mothers and daughters. Their primary achievements were endurance in the face of tragedy and an ability to inspire and encourage the men whose lives they touched. When women broke what Ellet's readers believed to be the bonds of prescribed femininity—when they killed enemy soldiers, rode unescorted through the night, spied on the enemy, or disguised themselves as men—Ellet defended their actions by referring to the extraordinary times. The Revolution, she argued, forced women to public deeds of bravery. Writing of one such woman, she declared: "It needed the trying scenes by which she was surrounded to develop the heroism which in times more peaceful, might have been unnoticed by those who knew her most intimately."

Ellet's message was clear: When her home was attacked, a woman might become "an Amazon in both strength and courage," rising to a challenge she could not avoid. Much like lionesses facing hunters, Revolutionary War era mothers would stop at nothing to protect their children from redcoats, "savages," or loyalists. And many a Revolutionary War era girl would gladly ride through dark forests and ford raging streams in order to warn a beloved father or brother of danger.[1]

Despite Ellet's genteel brushstrokes, she revealed a pride in the active patriotism of many of her subjects. Endurance, resignation, and loyalty were not, it seems, the whole story, and not all acts of bravery were prompted by dangers to family or home. Ellet's volumes also contain tales of women who dared to support the cause of independence—or to oppose it—on principle, just as men might do. These women risked their lives to protect a suspected spy, destroyed their crops to prevent the enemy from harvesting them, and sacrificed their homes to their chosen cause. And yet, the best of them, in Ellet's eyes, managed to engage in the political and military struggles without abandoning their feminine duties. Her deepest admiration, therefore, went to Mercy Otis Warren, the Massachusetts playwright, poet, and historian, who penned political satires in the 1760s and early 1770s that helped destroy the reputations and credibility of local Crown officials, and wrote what may have been the first history of the Revolution, yet never neglected her role as homemaker and mother.

Ellet's history was not a call for women's political equality. It did not advocate new roles for women outside the domestic sphere except in times of crisis. But Ellet did emphatically believe that the women who filled the pages of her books deserved to be remembered. Yet in the years following the Civil War, Ellet's books, like the women who were her subjects, were largely forgotten. By the 1880s, the writing of history had become a profession rather than a hobby or a passion, and it required credentials few women could attain. The new professional historians turned their attention to great men and formal politics, to generals and diplomats, to public figures and political institutions. The canvas they painted was too grand to include the small heroisms that Ellet had so carefully portrayed, and thus it was that a gendered amnesia befell the study of the nation's war for independence.[2]

Nevertheless, what might be called an "Ellet underground" continued to thrive among the organizations of descendants of the Revolutionary generation and among amateur local historians in towns, villages, and counties along the east coast. These women and men kept alive the stories of heroines—those who performed feats of bravery and those who preserved the farms and shops and families that soldiers dreamed of returning to when independence was won. Because of the efforts of these unabashed antiquarians, statues were erected to honor local heroines and medals were struck with the women's likenesses upon them. Women may have been absent from the formal narratives of the Revolution, but their stories were preserved.

For over one hundred years, the story of women's roles in American history was kept alive by this underground. But in the 1970s, the universities began producing women historians—and many of them chose to become historians of women. They set about the task of reconstructing women's experiences, confident that since Clio, the muse of history, was a woman, she would watch over her own kind. By the 1980s, the painstaking but often exhilarating task of restoring women to the canvas of American history had begun to reap rewards. New books and articles appeared that explored everything from the rise of Victorian sensibilities to the role of women in the textile mills of New England, from female abolitionists to advocates of woman suffrage. And Ellet and her women of the American Revolution slowly made their way back into the formal story of the nation's birth. It is the scholarship of these past few decades, as well as the work of amateur historians and antiquarians, that makes *Revolutionary Mothers* possible.[3]

One hundred and fifty-four years after Elizabeth Ellet's *Women of the Revolution*, this book retells the story of women's role in creating a new nation. And as much as possible, it tells that story through the words and actions of individual women—from Martha Washington to the Quaker spy Lydia Darragh, from the wealthy fund-raiser Esther DeBerdt Reed to the Indian diplomat Molly Brant.

Revolutionary Mothers is neither a romantic tale nor an effort to stand traditional history on its head by making women the central players in the war for independence. It does not tell one woman's story, but many, and not all of those stories end in triumph or victory. Instead, this book examines a war that continually blurred the lines between battlefield and home front, and it views that war through the eyes of the women who found themselves, willingly and unwillingly, at the center of a long and violent conflict. These women were neither generals nor statesmen. They played no formal role in declaring the war or making the peace. Yet women could hardly have been passive observers to a war waged in the streets of their towns and cities, in the fields of their family farms, or on their very doorsteps. The Revolution began with protests against taxation and a growing fear that Parliament and finally the king intended to enslave their own citizens. Women and girls were partners with their husbands, fathers, brothers, and sons in the public demonstrations against the new British policies and, if they were absent from the halls of the colonial legislatures, their presence was crucial in the most effective protest strategy of all: the boycott of British manufactured goods. As the war began, women transformed peacetime domestic chores and skills into wartime activities, becoming the unofficial quartermaster corps of the Continental Army and of their state regiments. Women traveled with the army—indeed, with both the British and the American armies—serving the men as cooks, laundresses, and nurses. On many occasions, they took a wounded husband's place at the cannon, and on a few occasions, they donned men's clothing and took up arms against the enemy troops. Women were enlisted to serve as spies and couriers for the king and for the revolutionaries. But more than anything else, wives and mothers and daughters kept farms and shops and families going for eight long years of conflict so that there was something to come home to when peace returned. It is these smaller acts of bravery, individual and collective, that constitute the heart of this book.

The long home-front war for American independence disrupted the normal life of every man and woman. It required them to adapt to a series of novel circumstances and pressing crises. They found themselves stepping out of familiar prescribed roles or engaging in traditional activities in untraditional settings. When men went off to fight the war, either on the battlefield or in the statehouses, women accepted the need to step in and direct household affairs, run the farm or shop, arm themselves against the enemy, and protect their families from danger. Although the tasks might be new, a long-standing gender expectation that women could act as "surrogate" or "deputy" husbands when necessary allowed most free white women to breach the walls dividing the feminine from the masculine without shattering their identities. How women thought about these experiences is part of the story told here.

Earlier generations of women had, of course, taken on many of these roles during the imperial wars between England and her rivals and in the midst of border strife between English settlers and Native Americans. They had faced inflation, shortages of essential supplies, widowhood, and the realities of death and destruction that came with violent conflict. But in the decade of protest before the Revolution and during the war itself, women entered a sphere largely unfamiliar to them: the world of politics. In the 1760s and 1770s, when the consumption of imported manufactured goods defined the colonial economy, their daily choices—to drink imported tea or to refuse it, to buy English cloth or to weave their own—became political acts. In the charged atmosphere of the day, they began to discuss political issues and declare political loyalties in newspapers and broadsides as well as in private conversation. While some male colonists criticized them for their boldness, far more urged them to continue. Yet, after the war, virtually no one suggested formalizing women's political participation, and women showed little interest in preserving the public platforms that newspapers had provided. In truth, most women seemed eager to return to the family roles they had known in more peaceful times. For them, the challenges of the extraordinary had been met only to preserve the survival of the ordinary. The return of women to their customary activities is yet another piece of the story.

Despite the absence of radical changes in gender ideology and gender roles for most women, the Revolution did lend legitimacy to new ideas about women's capacities and their proper roles. Although practice did not keep pace with theory, postwar society offered new opportunities for some women, and postwar intellectuals reinterpreted women's traditional roles in ways that eventually led to change. These shifts in perspective, whose implications were never fully recognized or realized by the Revolutionary War generation, are the final piece of this story.

The story of white patriotic women and the Revolution is only one story, of course, among several that need to be told. Both African American and Native American women came into the war with gender identities quite different from those of New England housewives or southern plantation mistresses. The war they helped to wage differed in its goals and its consequences from the war known as the Revolution to Pennsylvania or

Virginia matrons. In setting their stories apart, this book does not mean to imply that the lives of Indian and black women were not intertwined with those of white women, although the cords that bound them to the dominant culture were often cords of violence, exploitation, and oppression. Their stories are told separately in order to avoid treating them as detours, or deviations, from the dominant story and in order to ensure that their perceptions of events are not portrayed as a misunderstanding. For similar reasons, white loyalist women are the subject of a separate chapter. The protests of the 1760s and early 1770s drove a wedge between these women and their neighbors; the decision for independence led to the loss of their families' wealth and standing within their communities; and the American victory sent many of them into exile.

It is impossible to begin *Revolutionary Mothers* without a closer look at the lives and roles of the majority of women before Americans dreamed of independence and revolution. Thus the first chapter is prologue: a look at eighteenth-century English women in colonial society. It is also impossible to end the story with the signing of the peace treaty that made the colonies the United States of America. Thus the final chapter is epilogue: a look at the impact of war on gender roles and gender ideologies, on what was assumed to be "natural" in women and what was therefore natural for them to do.

CHAPTER 1

"THE EASY TASK OF OBEYING"

Englishwomen's Place in Colonial Society

There is a story told of John Winthrop, the first governor of the Massachusetts Bay Colony. One day in 1645, Governor Edward Hopkins of Connecticut consulted his friend Winthrop. Hopkins was greatly distressed, for his wife appeared to have completely lost her senses. Insanity had set in—without warning, he reported, and without apparent cause. Winthrop, however, instantly knew the origins of the woman's madness: reading books. "If she had attended her household affairs and such things as belong to women, and not gone out of her way and calling to meddle in such things as are proper to men, whose minds are stronger, etc.," he explained, then she might have "kept her wits."[1]

Few educated men of the following century would have made such a demeaning statement about a woman's intellect. Yet an equally small number were ready to concede that women, as much as men, had the capacity for rigorous formal education or political decision making. The

1

philosophers of the Enlightenment, whose works were so popular among the eighteenth-century colonial leadership, might insist that all humans had the ability to reason, but not even the most radical of these philosophers suggested that the fairer sex had abilities equal to those of men.

This debate over women's capacities was theoretical, of course, and few colonists, male or female, had the time or inclination to engage in it. Most colonial men and women—like most ordinary Americans today—took the gendered world as they found it, and, although what they found varied with social class and region, certain truths seemed too obvious to debate. Chief among a woman's truths was that God had created her to be a helpmate to man and Nature had formed her for this purpose. Her natural inclination was to obedience, fidelity, industriousness, and frugality and her natural function was bearing and nurturing children. From childhood, a woman heard her destiny as helpmate confirmed and affirmed by the authorities who peopled her world. Ministers sermonized it, educators elaborated it, lawmakers codified it, and poets versified it. From a pulpit in Massachusetts, the Puritan divine Cotton Mather urged a woman to be an "Ornament of Zion" by "look[ing] upon [a husband] as her guide" and recognizing that husband and wife are "but one mind in two bodies." In his 1712 book, *The Well Ordered Family,* the scholar Benjamin Wadsworth reminded women that God had made Eve as a helpmate to Adam and that the apostles required "wives be faithful in all things, keepers of the home." From the pages of his treatise *Baron and Feme,* Samuel Chase declared that "the law of nature has put [a wife] under the obedience of her husband," and the law of man must be made to agree. And, in his epic poem *Paradise Lost,* John Milton summed up the relationship between a husband and wife in an epigram of hierarchy: "He for God only / She for God in him."[2]

Thus, through precept, law, and custom, English society established the acceptable parameters of women's lives, just, of course, as it established those of men. On the whole, however, a woman's life was dominated by negatives. Born rich or poor, a woman faced restrictions on her economic independence, her legal identity, and her access to positions of formal authority. These restrictions nudged, or pushed, a woman into the narrow choice of marriage or spinsterhood. Colonial inheritance laws, drawn from English law, ensured her economic dependency, for sons were given land while daughters had to be content with movable property. Land ownership in colonial America defined a man as an independent citizen; the possession of cattle, slaves, and household goods defined a woman as a traveler from her father's house to her husband's. Sons might be apprenticed to learn skilled trades, brought into family businesses, or sent to college, but custom barred women from most crafts and the lingering belief that the female brain was too weak to absorb abstract ideas barred them from all but the most elementary education. Closed out of professions such as law and the ministry, landless, and with few acceptable occupations outside the household, most women who did not marry faced bleak futures as dependents in the homes of their parents or married sisters.

Spinsterhood was more than a life of dependency. It was more than a mark of rejection, a sign that men found a woman, in the blunt language of New England, a "thornback." Without a husband, a woman remained in limbo between childhood and adulthood, for English colonial society offered her no other rites of passage but marriage and motherhood. While men could chart their maturity by the call to militia service, by voting and perhaps office holding, by positions of honor within the church, or by landownership, all these public venues of responsibility were closed to women.

Marriage had its costs as well. As a *feme sole,* or woman alone, a colonial woman had access to a broader legal identity than she would as a matron. A *feme sole* could sue and be sued, earn what wages she could, buy and sell property, and will her assets to her heirs. Without these legal rights, a woman without family support would have become a burden on the state. Yet once a woman married, English society saw no need for her to enjoy these rights. In her new status as *feme covert,* or woman covered, all that she owned became her husband's property, even the clothes on her back. The noted English jurist Blackstone wrote lyrically of this deprivation, assuring new husbands that "by marriage, the husband and wife are one person in law: that is, the very being or legal existence of the woman is suspended during the marriage, or at least is incorporated and consolidated into that of the husband" and reassuring new wives that they were secure under their husbands' "wing, protection, and *cover.*"[3] In exchange for this complete surrender, the law guaranteed her dower rights, declaring that in widowhood she would have the use, though not the actual ownership, of one-third of her husband's property. Women might cherish dower rights as recognition of their contribution to the family welfare, but colonial governments saw this provision in more practical terms. A woman's "thirds" protected the state from the burden of caring for an aging woman or a young widow with children. If the law rendered a wife dependent, it also required a man to support her from the grave.

Colonial society ensured that women's identity was synonymous with the roles they played: wife and mother. Yet society could not ensure that the what and how of these roles remained uniform or constant. As the circumstances of women's lives grew more varied, the content of the roles changed. As cities grew, women adapted the repertoire of household skills to fit their urban lives. As social distinctions hardened, women of the upper classes adopted behavior that distinguished them from their poorer neighbors. Yet no matter how different the what and how, the why remained the same: women were helpmates to men.

In the seventeenth century, when the colonies were overwhelmingly rural and agricultural, the traditional skills a woman brought to the marriage—a repertoire of domestic manufacturing and processing skills—were essential to the success of the family. Her domain was the household, the garden, and the henhouse, and her days were spent processing the raw materials her husband produced into usable items such as food, clothing, candles, and soap. In this environment, a woman's fertility was as vital as her productivity, for children were an essential labor force on small farms throughout the colonies. Seventeenth-century gravestones and eulogies attested to the value placed on motherhood. Thus, women who hoped to gain renown in their small rural communities had to demonstrate a lifelong commitment to industry, frugality, and fecundity.

Rural housewives had little time for activities that the modern reader associates with housework: cleaning, dusting, polishing, and decorating. But in the colonial cities of the eighteenth century, among the growing ranks of prosperous mercantile families, these tasks now defined women's work. A consumer revolution—with its availability of cheap English cloth and the influx of luxury items that were now within the reach of the wealthy merchant or lawyer—had freed elite urban women from most production tasks. Able to purchase many of the goods their grandmothers had once made, these women turned their energies and attention to the refinement of their homes and of their families. With slaves or servants to assist them, and with greengrocers and bakers and seamstresses to supply their cupboards and their wardrobes, these "pretty gentlewomen," as one historian has called them, focused on the beautification of their homes and the genteel upbringing of their daughters. Along with this new set of chores came a new code of behavior, a new definition of femininity. Industry and frugality gave way to delicacy, refinement, and an attention to fashion. This new focus on gentility among the urban elite eliminated many housewifely activities, yet it also added others. Although they no longer churned butter or slaughtered pigs, these privileged women adopted a set of *maintenance* chores. Cleanliness became a mark of urban sophistication, and even when servants or slaves performed the unpleasant tasks of scouring, laundering, and polishing, the burden of ensuring an attractive domestic environment fell squarely upon their mistresses.[4]

Many women found themselves caught between the older ideal of "notable housewife" and the newer ideal of "pretty gentlewoman," and thus shouldering the burdens of gentility and the burdens of traditional housewifery. Thus, in addition to planting her garden and pickling her beef, Mary Holyoke, the wife of a prosperous country doctor, felt compelled to scour the pewter and hang pictures. In her daybook, Holyoke carefully recorded her workweek: "Washed. Ironed. Scoured pewter. Scoured rooms. Scoured furniture Brasses and put up the chintz bed and hung pictures. Sowed Sweet marjoram. Sowed pease. Sowed cauliflower. Sowed 6 week beans. Pulled radishes. Set out turnips. Cut 36 asparagus. Killed the pig, weighed 164 pounds. Made bread. Put beef in pickle. Salted Pork, put bacon in pickle. Made the Dr. [her husband] 6 cravats marked H. Quilted two petticoats since yesterday. Made 5 shirts for the doctor." Her diary entry ends with this remarkable understatement: "did other things."[5]

Occasionally we can catch glimpses of the frustration women felt as they struggled to satisfy the demands of housewifery and gentility. After two days of midsummer cherry harvesting, spring house cleaning, and a hog butchering, Mary Cooper of Oyster Bay, New York, recorded that she was "full of fretting discontent dirty and miserable both yesterday and today." A year later, her discontent resurfaced: "It has been a tiresome day it is now Bedtime and I have not had won minutts rest." At last, in October 1768, Cooper offered this modest eighteenth-century version of "a room of one's own": "I have the blessing to be quite alone without any Body greate or small . . ."[6]

In the pursuit of gentility, both men and women

8

embraced a concern with personal appearance—not simply how they looked but how they behaved in polite society. They devoured English advice manuals that prescribed and proscribed behavior, providing step-by-step instructions on everything from proper dress to regulating the decibel levels of one's speech. Mothers labored to instruct their children in the complicated, subtle rules of refinement. Through a steady regimen of social calls, elaborate tea parties, dances, and balls, women honed a new set of skills that would earn them notability.

A suitable marriage was, of course, the raison d'être behind a young woman's mastery of dancing, fine needlework, and French. Wealthy girls understood that "a woman's happiness depends entirely on the husband she is united to." In their letters and diaries, genteel girls set high standards for behavior and character in the men they considered eligible suitors, sensible, as one wrote, "that Happiness does not consist of Wealth, but the Riches of the Mind." Their mothers and fathers were often more practical. For the parents of romantic young girls, a man's assets had to include wealth and property as well as an ability to be pleasing "both in person and Conversation."[7]

Nothing in this new credo of gentility challenged the subordination of women to men. For if women were now to be charming companions to their husbands rather than useful workers, their purpose remained to satisfy male expectations for a wife. As a wife, even the most refined woman understood her place. "Making it the business of my life to please a man of Mr. Pinckney's merit even in triffles," wrote Eliza Lucas Pinckney in 1742, "I esteem a pleasing task; and I am well assured the acting out of my proper province and invading his, would be an inexcusable breach of prudence; as his superior understanding . . . would point him to dictate, and leave me nothing but the easy task of obeying."[8]

The ideal woman of the farmhouse—obedient, faithful, frugal, fertile, and industrious—or the ideal woman of the eighteenth-century parlor—obedient, charming, chaste, and modest—was rarely fully realized. In the very heart of John Winthrop's early New England, wives were known to batter their husbands, commit adultery, abandon their families, and murder their newborn infants. Women were enjoined to "submit yourselves unto your own husbands as unto the Lord," yet local newspapers carried a small but steady stream of notices that a wife had "not only eloped from my Bed and Board, but otherwise behaves in a very unbecoming manner toward me." Women's bodies moved to the rhythms of pregnancy, childbirth, nursing, and weaning, but court records in every colony preserve instances of abortion, infanticide, and incest. Ministers praised chaste brides, yet women in the eighteenth century, as in the seventeenth, were often pregnant when they took their vows. Although husbands were urged to "love your wives, and be not bitter against them," men were known to vent their anger in their wills at a lifetime spent with a slovenly wife, a shrew, or a cold, unloving partner. And despite all the incentives society offered women to marry, some single women and some prosperous widows refused to give up the freedom they enjoyed in their husbandless state. Poets like Anne Bradstreet could write movingly of her marriage as a perfect union, declaring, "If ever two were one, then surely we / If ever man were loved by wife, then thee"; almost a century later, Abigail Adams could assure her husband, John, that "the Affection I feel for my Friend is of the tenderest kind." But an anonymous poet cheerfully declared, "I'll never marry, no indeed / For marriage causes trouble; / And after all the priest has said, / 'Tis merely hubble bubble."[9]

Despite evidence that individual colonists defied social expectations, rejected social norms, and honored religious principles and precepts in the breach, there was no concerted effort to replace them, no carefully crafted public critique of them. Runaway wives and abusive husbands were responding to the same gender ideals and gender roles as notable housewives, genteel matrons, and their husbands. As a modern observer might put it, they remained within the paradigm.

Women's helpmate role persisted throughout the colonial period, in part because it faced no serious challenge, and in part because of its adaptability to new circumstances and its adjustment to new contexts. Even the most traditional form of helpmate could be stretched to accommodate the unusual circumstances that arose in English colonial America. Thus, although the English endorsed a gendered division of labor, with men in the fields and shops and women in the home and its immediate environs, wives and daughters were often called upon to help with a planting or a harvest or to keep a record of an artisan husband's accounts. On the fringes of settlement, where Indians and colonists clashed, women wielded muskets and knives, sharing the role of protector in their family and community. Husbands, away on business, serving in the military, or appearing in court, left their wives to oversee farm or shop and family. If husbands died before their sons reached maturity, their widows were often entrusted to manage the family's assets, operating the shop or the farm until sons reached adulthood. Yet no matter how long her caretaking duties lasted, no matter how hard she labored in the fields, no matter how ferocious she became in frontier warfare or steadfast in captivity, these actions did not blur the line between male and female. Instead, colonists broadened the definition of helpmate to include a woman's temporary duties as a deputy or surrogate husband. Thus when wives stepped into their husbands' shoes, performing male duties, exhibiting masculine traits such as bravery or aggressiveness, the gender lines remained intact; for radical though their actions might be, these women were fulfilling their obligations as helpmate.

The Revolution, however, stretched to its limits this notion of woman as helpmate and surrogate husband. As protest against English policies mounted, women began to test their political voice. "We commenced perfect statesmen," wrote one southerner; across the colonies, women and girls developed concerns outside the private world of the family and began to "think nationly." And, as the war dragged on, the women who managed the farms and the shops grew to think of themselves as proprietors rather than custodians. Yet the deprivations and the horrors of war bore down on them, and a longing for a return to the life they knew grew within them, too. This battle between familiar roles and new ones was part of the war waged by women. And it all began with a protest over stamps and tea.

CHAPTER 2

"THEY SAY IT IS TEA THAT CAUSED IT"

Women Join the Protest Against English Policy

The year was 1765 and in the halls of colonial legislatures from Massachusetts to the Carolinas, leaders rose to protest the disturbing signs that their rights as Englishmen were being threatened. In the newspapers and on the streets of colonial cities, cries of "No taxation without representation!" could be heard as crowds threatened royal officials and destroyed their property. Almost overnight, the wave of nationalism that had followed Britain's stunning victory in the French and Indian Wars gave way to suspicion and anger. Only two years earlier, colonists had lifted their glasses to toast the majesty of their young king George III, the strategic genius of William Pitt, and the heroism of the fallen General James Wolfe. They had celebrated the end to almost a century of intermittent warfare and the horrors of Indian raids on the colonial borders, and they had looked with pride on the fact that the tyrannical yoke of France had been lifted from Canada and the Ohio Valley.

Yet the sweet taste of victory had soured quickly. Land-hungry colonists saw their hopes dashed in 1763 when Parliament proclaimed territory west of the Appalachians off-limits until a coherent Indian policy could be developed. The following year, New England shippers and merchants grew indignant when the British government's American Revenue Act signaled a crackdown on their profitable smuggling of foreign sugar into mainland ports. And, now, in a move that shocked colonists everywhere, Parliament had usurped the prerogatives of their colonial assemblies and passed a direct tax on vital services and basic goods. The Stamp Act of 1765 required that government-issued stamps be placed on all legal documents and newspapers as well as playing cards and dice. In one ill-advised stroke, the mother country managed to anger not only local political leaders, but also the most vocal members of colonial society—its lawyers and editors—and those most likely to take their protest to the streets—sailors, dockworkers, and other members of the growing colonial urban poor. This threat to local government's control over taxation also managed to produce what the threat of Indian attack and French invasion had not: united political action by the colonies. Even before the hated stamps arrived in America, the hastily called Stamp Act Congress had agreed to a boycott of all British-made goods until the tax was repealed.

American women were not present in the halls

of the Virginia House of Burgesses as the great orator Patrick Henry rose to protest the tyrannical yoke not of France but of Parliament. They did not gather in the dockside taverns of Boston where the wily Samuel Adams helped transform the city's local gangs into the Sons of Liberty. And their opinions were not sought when delegates to the Stamp Act Congress composed their arguments against direct taxation, penned their petitions to Parliament, and decided on their strategy to force the act's repeal. But when the call went out for a boycott of British goods, women became crucial participants in the first organized opposition to British policy.

Thus, the first political act of American women was to say "No." In cities and small towns, women said no to merchants who continued to offer British goods and no to the consumption of those goods, despite their convenience or appeal. Their "no"s had an immediate and powerful effect, for women had become major consumers and purchasers by the mid-eighteenth century. And in American cities, widows, wives of sea captains and sailors, and unmarried women who ran their own shops had to make the decision to say no to selling British goods. In New York City a group of brides-to-be said no to their fiancés, putting a public notice in the local newspaper that they would not marry men who applied for a stamped marriage license.[1]

Parliament could ignore the assemblies' petitions.

It could turn a deaf ear to soaring oratory and flights of rhetoric. But Parliament could not withstand the pressures placed on it by English merchants and manufacturers who saw their sales plummet and their warehouses overflow because of the boycott. In March 1766, the Stamp Act was repealed.

Over the next few years, Parliament looked frantically for new means to extract revenue from the colonies. While many colonists became convinced of a plot to destroy American prosperity or to reduce freeborn citizens to slaves, the British government saw these measures as a practical response to wartime and postwar budget problems. As a succession of prime ministers quickly learned, the British government was in desperate financial straits. England had borrowed heavily to wage its long war against France, and it faced continued military expenses if it hoped to keep what it had won. Since the English taxpayers were demanding relief from wartime levels of taxation and were in no mood to see their burden increased, the only possible new source of revenue was the colonies.

A sympathetic colonist might see the logic, or the justice, in Parliament's decision to enforce old trade restrictions and impose new ones, but there were few sympathetic colonists to be found. Thus, in 1767, when the British chancellor of the exchequer, Charles Townshend, tried to expand import duties to include British-made goods such as paper, paint, and tea, colonists were quick to organize opposition once again. The campaign to repeal the Stamp Act had taught them valuable lessons: united action was more effective than individual responses, and nonimportation and non-consumption were the most powerful weapons in their arsenal of resistance.

The boycott that followed covered items as luxurious as "Coaches, Chaises and Carriages of all Sorts" and as basic as "Cordage, Anchors . . . Linseed Oyle [and] Glue." And, once again, women were asked to wield their purchasing power as a political weapon. Local boycott committees put pressure on women to abstain from purchasing sugar, gloves, hats, ready-made clothing, a great variety of fabrics, and shoes, while newspapers carried poems assuring women that they would be more attractive to men if they refrained from drinking British tea. "Throw aside your Bohea and your Green Hyson Tea," wrote one wit in 1767, promising that "though the times remain darkish, young men may be sparkish / And love you much stronger than ever."[2]

For a small but growing number of women, quiet acquiesence to the boycott did not seem to be enough. In Boston, there were women who preferred to issue manifestos of their own. Such action was not without risk to their reputations. Women's names rarely appeared in print, unless they were runaway servants, brides, or merchants or craftswomen advertising their wares. Genteel women were rarely discussed in print except in eulogies. Despite the risk, on February 12, 1770, the *Boston Evening Post* carried the names of "upwards of 300 Mistresses of Families, in which Number the Ladies of the highest Rank and Influence" who had signed an agreement to "join with the very respectable Body of Merchants and other Inhabitants of this Town who met in Fanueil Hall" and pledged to abstain from the use of tea. "Join with" implied independent decision making rarely displayed by "Ladies." Almost one hundred other women from the less prosperous section of town "of their own free will and accord" announced they had written and signed their own boycott agreement.[3]

Public opinion seemed to favor this new daring on the part of women. Yet women who wished to do more than put their names on a petition proceeded with caution. When Mercy Otis Warren, sister of one of Massachusetts' leading radicals and wife of another, decided to write a series of stinging satirical plays about local royal officials, she published them anonymously. Friends like John Adams reveled in the damage that her characterizations did to the reputations of such royal office-holders as Governor Thomas Hutchinson or Attorney General Jonathan Sewall, who supported British policies. Yet Warren consistently denied her authorship of these plays, even to Adams. When the poet Hannah Griffitts wrote urging Pennsylvania women to support the boycott, she too published her work anonymously. Anonymity not only allowed

Griffitts to maintain her genteel reputation; it allowed her to openly criticize Pennsylvania men for failing to enforce the boycott themselves:

> *Since the men, from a party or fear of a frown*
> *Are kept by a sugar-plum quietly down*
> *Supinely asleep—and depriv'd of their sight*
> *Are stripp'd of their freedom, and robb'd of their*
>   *right;*
> *If the sons, so degenerate! the blessings despise*
> *Let the Daughters of Liberty nobly arise.*[4]

Anonymous verses continued to appear in colonial newspapers, many of them urging women to politicize their daily domestic life. What a woman bought when she went to a shop, what she ate, what she drank, and the clothing she chose to wear could all signal a political commitment as well as a personal choice. A popular verse advised women to

> *First, then, throw aside your topknots of pride,*
> *Wear none but your own country linen;*
> *Of economy boast, let your pride be the most*
> *To show clothes of your own make and spinning.*[5]

"Clothes of your own make and spinning," or homespun, quickly became a badge of honor and a visible political statement. Thirteen-year-old Anna Green Winslow articulated the connection clearly: "As I am (as we say) a daughter of liberty,

I chuse to war as much of our own manufactory as possible." Winslow's identification of herself as a "daughter of liberty" placed her in the growing ranks of women who felt "nationly." Urged by the press, by ministers, and by the colonial leadership to look upon domestic duties and chores as political weapons, these women began to see themselves, for the first time, as actors upon the political stage. This new role, as a political actor rather than an observer, was not easily assumed. Among women of the genteel classes, it clashed with the image of delicacy and femininity they had cultivated. Twenty-two-year-old Charity Clarke voiced her uneasiness in a series of letters to a male friend in England. She feared, she wrote, that her discussion of politics would destroy the "Idea you have of [my] female softness." Yet she could not remain silent. The vision Clarke conjured up of a "fighting army of Amazones," ready to do battle for colonial rights, may have been a flight of fancy, but her willingness to see an independent, self-sufficient America marked her as decidedly more radical than most of the political leadership in 1769. That June, she had issued a warning to her friend:

> If you English folks won't give us the liberty we ask . . . I will try to gather a number of ladies armed with spinning wheels [along with men] who shall all learn to weave & keep sheep, and will retire beyond the reach of arbitrary power, cloathed with the work

21

of our hands, feeding on what the country affords. . . . In short, we will found a new Arcadia.[6]

Clarke's new Arcadia was far from the minds of most colonists, but a campaign to become self-sufficient was mounted in New England. Here, spinning wheels were brought out and dusted off, and lessons in what had become a lost art were offered. Notices of spinning bees for those who remembered how to do it, and of spinning demonstrations for those who had never sat at a wheel, began to appear in local newspapers. Many of these events were hosted by local ministers. Most of the women who participated were unmarried—daughters of prosperous families who were, as one historian has put it, America's first leisure class, yet some wives and mothers managed to attend, despite their household and child-care duties. A matron from Brookfield, New Hampshire, for example, did "the morning work of a large family, made her cheese, etc, and then rode more than two miles, and carried her own wheel, and sat down to spin at nine in the morning, and by seven in the evening spun 53 knots" before "she went home to milking."[7]

Unlike Anna Winslow, many of the women who joined these spinning bees may not have seen themselves as "daughters of liberty." Instead, they may have viewed their actions in more traditional terms, as acts of charity for the poor, the widowed, and the ailing, upon whom the boycott of English cloth fell as a special burden. Yet they could not prevent other colonists from interpreting their actions in more radical terms. The women had, after all, transformed what was traditionally a solitary activity into a group effort. They had crammed dozens of bulky machines and dozens of women into the modest space of a minister's home, and their spinning sessions had been publicly advertised. It was not surprising, therefore, that their personal motivations were lost in the outpouring of praise—and condemnation—that followed what others saw as a conscious political act. Peter Oliver, who would later prefer exile to rebellion, believed that the ministers had consciously inflamed these women into acts of rebellion. "The dissenting Clergy, were . . . set to Work, to preach up Manufactures instead of Gospel," Oliver later wrote in his history of the Revolution. "They preached about it . . . until the Women & Children, both within Doors & without, set their Spinning Wheels a whirling in Defiance of *Great Britain.*" But supporters of the boycott believed the women needed no outside encouragement; their spinning bees were evidence of their own "love of Liberty, and strict Attachment to their Country's Welfare." Newspaper commentators heaped praise upon the spinners, insisting, as one contributor to the *Boston Evening Post* put it, "that the industry and frugality of American ladies must exalt their character in the Eyes of the

World and serve to show how greatly they are contributing to bring about the political salvation of a whole Continent."[8]

Once again, nonimportation and nonconsumption helped force the repeal of the British revenue-raising effort. But the tensions between mother country and colonies did not ease. In Boston and New York, the arrival of British regulars, or redcoats, sent to squelch further riots and demonstrations against British policy and to protect royal officeholders only led to violence between civilians and soldiers. In 1770, a confrontation between British troops and Boston citizens left five men dead. When a local silversmith, Paul Revere, rushed into print an engraving of the evening's violence, this compelling piece of propaganda, with its image of ruthless British soldiers firing on an innocent crowd, persuaded men and women throughout the colonies that the event was a massacre. Although calm seemed to settle over the colonies after the "Boston Massacre," political leaders and writers continued to examine the relationship between Parliament and the assemblies and to raise disturbing questions about their future within the empire. In pamphlets, speeches, and private letters, they parsed out the obligations and privileges of the government and its citizens and gauged what they considered to be the erosion of colonial rights. To an increasing number of colonists, the British government's aggressive policies seemed to reflect a society mired in corruption and mismanagement. Neither men nor women talked yet of independence or rebellion, but as the decade of the glorious victory over France ended, a general wariness colored the thoughts of many colonists. Only this growing mistrust could have sparked the tempest in a teapot that began in 1773.

American colonists, like their English counterparts, took their tea drinking seriously, consuming great quantities in much the same fashion as modern Americans drink coffee. Although the East India Tea Company, a British enterprise, technically held a monopoly on the American trade, Dutch traders had regularly captured much of the colonial market by offering lower prices. Two factors had kept the price of English tea high. First, colonists paid a middleman fee to the English merchants who re-exported the tea to America. Secondly, when Parliament repealed the Townshend duties, they kept the import tax on the tea as a symbol of their right to legislate for the colonies. In 1773, a mismanaged and floundering East India Tea Company came to Parliament, hoping for legislation that would bail them out. Parliament soon came up with a plan to make the company's tea more attractive to the colonial market. The Tea Act of 1773 allowed the company to eliminate the English merchant middlemen and sell directly to the colonists. Even with the tea tax still in effect, English tea would now be cheaper than its competitor.

The British government anticipated few complaints over the new arrangement, and may, in fact, have expected their decision to be greeted warmly. It was not. Parliament had once again underestimated colonial mistrust and colonial readiness to resist any further erosion of their rights. Rumors quickly spread that Parliament intended to drive out foreign teas, assure the East India Company a monopoly on the universally popular drink, and then allow the company to drastically raise its prices. Many colonists believed the Tea Act was an excuse to collect the tax on tea and thus establish a precedent for new taxes on British goods. Almost no one saw it for what it probably was: a tactic to save a company in which several leading members of Parliament had invested.

Drinking, or refusing to drink, tea immediately became the new litmus test of colonial patriotism. And once again, much of the burden seemed to fall on women. In South Carolina, the Presbyterian minister William Tennent III insisted that women could save the colonies "from the Dagger of Tyranny" if they gave up the "trivial pleasure" of drinking tea. "Yes ladies," he declared, "You have it in your power more than all your committees and Congresses, to strike the Stroke, and make the Hills and Plains of America clap their hands." Though caught up in his own oratory, Tennent clearly recognized the psychological, if not the economic, impact of female political action. When the British saw that "American patriotism extends even to the Fair Sex," Parliament would feel compelled to end its oppression. Tennent's tone might strike the modern reader as patronizing, and his warning that every cup of tea sipped by women would be "paid for by the Blood of your sons" as histrionic, but to his eighteenth-century audience his message was both sound and radical: once again women's daily domestic activity was equally, or more, important to the colonial future than the actions of male congresses and assemblies.[9]

The women of North Carolina accepted the challenge to make the hills of their colony clap their hands. On October 25, 1774, some ten months after Boston radicals dumped a cargo of British tea into their harbor, fifty-one women gathered at the Edenton home of Elizabeth King. Constituting themselves as the Edenton Ladies' Patriotic Guild, they composed and signed an agreement to boycott all British-made goods and products. "As we cannot be indifferent on any occasion that appears nearly to affect the peace and happiness of our country," they wrote, "and as it has been thought necessary, for the public good, to enter into several resolves by a meeting of members deputed from the whole province, it is a duty which we owe, not only to our near and dear connections, who have concurred in them, but to ourselves, who are essentially interested in their welfare, to do everything, as far as lies in our power, to testify our sincere adherence to the same; and we do therefore accordingly subscribe this paper as a witness of our fixed intentions and solemn determination to do so." Their pledge was widely published in the colonies and appeared in the English *Morning Chronicle and London Advertiser* on January 16, 1775.[10]

The Edenton Resolves illustrated perfectly the liminal state of women's political identity. These North Carolina women had traveled from surrounding towns and farms for the sole purpose of issuing a public declaration. Yet in the preface accompanying that declaration, they carefully acknowledged that they were following "the laudable example of their husbands." And in the brief but dramatic resolution itself, the Edenton ladies declared that they acted out of a duty to the husbands and family who shared their patriotism. Yet they also declared that it was a duty they owed to themselves. In the end, their resolution went beyond a show of support for their husbands. It was a civic act, a commitment to the larger realm of "the public good." Their resolve, both as a character trait and as a document, carried the women beyond the role of surrogate husband or dutiful wife. But it did not carry them into full autonomy.

The Edenton Ladies Agreement seemed to conservative men to signal the same social anarchy as the Boston Tea Party's destruction of private property. Writing to his brother James from England, Arthur Iredell mocked the entrance of women into the public, political sphere. "Is there a female Congress at Edenton too?" he asked. "I hope not, for we Englishmen are afraid of the Male Congress, but if the Ladies, who have ever, since the Amazonian Era, been esteemed the most formidable Enemies, if they, I say, should attack us, the most fatal consequences is to be dreaded." Iredell's Amazon imagery was far less romantic than Charity Clarke's had been; his reference conjured up masculinized, aberrant women, dangerous and out of control. Fortunately, he continued, the Edenton ladies were indeed aberrant, for in all probability there were "but few of the places in America, who possess so much female Artillery as Edenton."[11]

Iredell was more right than he knew. For, despite the political daring of the Edenton women or the vocal support of the boycotts by Boston matrons, there were many women—and men—who remained mere observers of the conflict forming around them. Temperance Smith, a parson's wife from Sharon, Connecticut, spoke for many women when she said she was simply too busy to complain about "extra duties." "To tell the truth, I had no leisure for murmuring," she wrote. "I rose with the sun and all through the long day I had no time for aught but my work. So much did it press upon me that I could scarcely divert my thoughts from its demands." And while some women could clearly articulate the principle of "no taxation without representation," just as many were like Jemima Condict, a New Jersey farm girl, who had only a vague understanding of the issues that seemed to be moving the colonies toward war. "It seems we have troublesome times acoming," she wrote in her diary in October 1774, "for there is a great disturbance abroad in the earth, and they say it is tea that caused it. So then, if they will quarrel about such a trifling thing as that, what must we expect but war?"[12]

The "quarrel about such a trifling thing" was rapidly escalating in New England. After the destruction of the tea, the British government determined to teach Massachusetts in general, and Boston in particular, a lesson in obedience. The strategy was simple: to isolate this troublemaking colony and to crush its rebellious spirit. In rapid succession, Parliament's Intolerable Acts altered the provincial charter, closed the ports, changed legal procedures, and, to ensure that its punishments were enforced, removed the civilian governor and replaced him with General Thomas Gage. But the rebellious spirit had spread more widely than the king or the Parliament realized. In Virginia and the Carolinas, in New York and Pennsylvania, defiant colonists put together shipments of supplies for the besieged Bostonians. The rhetoric in newspapers and pamphlets grew more militant, as political writers declared Parliament an enemy of colonial rights and liberties. The most radical among them urged colonists to arm themselves against British attack.

In September 1774, political leaders from every colony but Georgia gathered in Philadelphia at the first Continental Congress. Although many delegates urged caution and compromise rather than revolution, the congress refused to offer an olive branch to the king; instead, they demanded the repeal of the Intolerable Acts and called for a third boycott of British goods.

The firm stand taken by this Continental Congress was a culmination of a decade of questioning, debating, and re-evaluating the colonial relationship to the mother country. In their insistence on the rights of local assemblies to govern internal affairs, colonial leaders had slowly redrawn the political map of the empire in their minds. They had renounced parliamentary supremacy and substituted a radical division of sovereignty in which the assemblies governed the colonies with the same authority that Parliament governed England. Only a shared loyalty to the Crown welded these separate parts of the empire into an imperial whole. Not surprisingly, neither Parliament nor the king accepted this reinterpretation. Attitudes in England had hardened since the destruction of the tea and the few outspoken advocates of colonial rights had lost ground in Parliament. By 1774, the government was determined to assert its sovereignty over *all* British citizens.

Outside the halls of government, the lines drawn between what came to be known as colonial loyalists and colonial patriots had also hardened. Violence erupted as radical men and women tried to pressure their neighbors into supporting colonial resistance. These crowds targeted women as well as men. The loyalist newspaper *Rivington's Gazette* reported in early 1775 that a mob had attacked a private gathering of women, flinging "stones which broke the shutters and windows and endangered their lives." Women who had expressed no political views but were wives or daughters of loyalists were not spared condemnation for "basely and cowardly [giving] up the public cause of freedom." A Massachusetts loyalist described the patriot women in these crowds as caught up in "a certain epidemical phrenzy" that surpassed "all the pretended patriotic virtue of the more robustic males." Peter Oliver, who found it "highly diverting" to see poor widows of Boston sign boycott agreements on luxury items such as silk or velvet or clock, and wealthy women stock up on tea *before* they embraced the ban, was appalled by the presence of women in mobs that tarred and feathered vocal supporters of the Crown. The breach of feminine restraint and delicacy seemed to him almost as radical as the rebellion itself. "When a Woman throws aside her Modesty," he wrote, "Virtue drops a tear." Patriots disagreed. Ezra Stiles, the future president of Yale, applauded news of New England women who "surpassed the men for Eagerness & Spirit in the Defence of Liberty by Arms." Female virtue was clearly in the eyes of the beholder.[13]

In early 1775, King George III escalated the war of words into a war of musket and rifle. Convinced that a few rabble-rousers in Massachusetts were behind all the trouble in his colonies, the king ordered General Gage to arrest Samuel Adams and John Hancock. Gage dutifully ordered redcoats into the Massachusetts countryside on the evening of April 18. Paul Revere and William Dawes rode out immediately to warn the two men and to alert local militiamen that British regulars were on their way. Before the night was over, "the shot heard round the world" was fired on Lexington Green. The war Jemima Condict feared had unofficially begun. If she now felt herself forced to make a political commitment, there were women who were eager to declare their loyalties. One of these was Esther deBerdt Reed of Philadelphia. That October, several months before Tom Paine's *Common Sense* broke the last bonds of loyalty to the king for many Americans, Reed wrote proudly to her brother in England that her cause, and her husband's cause, was "liberty and virtue, how much soever it may be branded by the names of rebellion and treason." Beneath her strong and determined tone, however, lay a fear of what the future held in store. "We have a powerful enemy to contend with," she conceded, adding, "Everything that is dear to us is at stake."[14] In the coming months, Reed would discover how right she was.

CHAPTER 3

"YOU CAN FORM NO IDEA OF THE HORRORS"

The Challenges of a Home-Front War

On April 4, 1775, Boston's leading propagandist for the colonial cause, Mercy Otis Warren, wrote to John Adams of the "dark and Gloomy aspect of public affairs." Can a peaceful resolution to the problems between the colonies and the Mother Country be found, she asked, or "must the Blood of the Best Citizens be poured out to Glut the Vengeance of the most Worthless and Wicked men?" Two weeks later, Warren had her answer. On April 18, 1775, riders passed through the towns outside of Boston, their urgent shouts of "To arms! To arms!" breaking the silence of a spring evening. As Massachusetts men poured out of their homes, frightened children and worried women remained behind to endure the terrible suspense of waiting.

By the end of the day, "the shot heard round the world" had been fired and an undeclared revolution had begun. The following month, Abigail Adams wrote to her husband, then far away at the

Continental Congress, that their own town of Braintree expected "soon to be in continual alarms." Rumors of attacks by the British had spread, she explained, and "We know not what a day will bring forth, nor what distress one hour may throw us into." In the face of such un-certainty, the usually steady Abigail feared that the "calmness and presence of Mind" she took pride in might falter during John's absence.[1]

For Abigail Adams, and for American women everywhere, the hours and days and years that followed were indeed filled with distress. For the war would bring problems of inflation, scarcity, and the threat of physical violence to their towns and to their doorsteps. During the course of the American Revolution, many women would confront these wartime problems alone, for their fathers, husbands, and sons were in military ser-vice. The Revolution was not the first war, of course, in which women faced these challenges. Frequent warfare between England and its rivals and frontier conflicts with Native Americans had left impoverished widows and struggling young mothers in their wake. These wars had left homes in ruin and families destroyed by capture or imprisonment or death. But this war was different. This time Americans could not hope for the protection of a mighty British navy or well-trained British troops, for the military power of the mother country was now aligned against them. This time, shortages were not simply a by-product of war but a conscious policy, for the source of the supplies and provisions Americans desperately needed was now the enemy. This time the violence was not confined to one border area or to one surprise raid on an isolated settlement. This was a home-front war, fought in the countryside and in the city streets of every colony-turned-state, leaving few safe havens from the confusion, destruction, and atrocities that came with occupying armies. And this was a civil war, pitting neighbor against neighbor as well as colonist against Crown. In these circumstances, it was difficult enough for women to continue to perform their familiar domestic duties. It was daunting to take on the duties of their absent husbands as well. Yet even as they struggled to maintain the farm or shop, to protect their children and their homes, they were also being asked to expand their circle of affection and interest beyond their family to the civic realm.

The immediacy of this war pressed upon the minds of many American women. Lexington and Concord, after all, were not frontier settlements, and British-occupied Boston was a major American port. For women living in coastal towns or long-settled country villages, for women on tidewater plantations or in the wheat-rich counties of eastern Pennsylvania, war had been, until now, a distant nightmare, waged on contested lands on Massachusetts's northern border, in sparsely settled western New York, in the Ohio

Valley, or in the backcountry of the Carolinas. Suddenly, the battlefield was the long-established seaport towns of Massachusetts. Who was safe if British soldiers, returning from skirmishes with colonial minutemen, could force their way into the Cambridge home of Hannah Adams, the wife of Deacon Joseph Adams, and, putting a bayonet to her breast, threaten to kill her? Where could a woman escape the dangers of battle if her "leg was shot of at her ancle by a cannonball" while she hid in her house during the battle of Trenton in 1777? How could a woman protect her home if an occupying British army could enter a farmhouse and destroy "Tables chairs looking glases and Picture Frames"?[2]

Once begun, the war seemed to spread rapidly, reaching from Boston to Philadelphia, New York, Norfolk, and Charleston and into the farmlands to the west even before independence had been formally declared. Within a year of the battle of Bunker Hill, British warships had filled the harbor of the second largest colonial city, New York, and British troops had raised their country's flag over the city itself. In January 1776, Virginia's governor had issued a call to African American slaves to rebel against their masters, and British ships bombarded Norfolk, injuring and killing women and children as well as men. Soon the British would mount the first of two major campaigns that would devastate the South. "War in itself however distant is indeed terrible," wrote sixteen-year-old Betsy

Ambler of Virginia, "but when brought to our very doors, when those we most love are personally engaged in it, when our friends and neighbors are exposed to its ravages . . . the reflection is overwhelming." That the war might, indeed, eventually come to a woman's "very doors" was enough to unnerve even the most confident of women throughout the country. When Eliza Wilkinson, the daughter of a wealthy planter, first learned that British troops were nearing her father's plantation southeast of Charleston, she confessed: "I did not know what to think, much less what to do . . . Thousands would I have given to have been in any part of the globe where I might not see them . . ."[3]

Even when the battlefield remained far away, the war's impact was immediate. Enlistment campaigns both for local regiments and the emerging Continental Army began soon after Lexington and Concord. Men and women responded differently to the call to arms—at least this seemed to be the case to one of the revolutionary leaders of South Carolina, William Moultrie. Listening to the minister deliver a rousing recruitment sermon at the South Carolina Provincial Congress on February 17, 1777, Moultrie observed that the men's passions were stirred but the women were "affected quite in a different way." He watched as "floods of tears rolled down their cheeks, from the sad reflection of their nearest and dearest friends and relations entering into a dreadful civil war." What seemed to sadden these women most was that the loss of life "could not be avoided." For some, the reality of the violence and death to come was simply too much to bear. After Faith Trumbull Huntington, daughter of the governor of Connecticut, witnessed the carnage of the battle of Bunker Hill, she abandoned all notions of the "pomp and circumstance of glorious war." Her brother, John Trumbull, noted sadly that the realization of the danger and hardship ahead for her husband and brothers "overcame her strong, but too sensitive mind." Faith Huntington, he wrote, "became deranged, and died the following November."[4]

While war songs might insist that "Husbands must leave their loving wives / And sprightly youths attend / Leave their sweethearts and risk their lives / Their country to defend," some women, especially poorer women, resented the feelings of patriotism that carried their husbands and sons off to war. "I was troubled to think," wrote Hannah Robertson after her husband enlisted, "that he should love to be going so much in the war and leave me with helpless children in very poor circumstances." Others railed against recruiting officers who they accused of luring their husbands away.[5]

Yet there were also women who encouraged American men to enlist. Following the pattern set down in the years of the boycotts, these women issued public statements and appeals in the newspapers, urging other wives to let their husbands go. In September 1776, Anne Terrel of Virginia published a letter in the *Virginia Gazette,* testifying to her willingness to see "the tenderest of husbands" leave home to fight and calling on female readers to do the same.[6]

For other women, the issue was not whether their men would enlist, but how they would acquit themselves in uniform. The traditional connection between manliness and physical bravery, between patriotism and sacrifice, made the battlefield a test of masculinity. Its corollary was that a woman could neither respect nor love a man unwilling to face danger. A popular poem captured this notion: "Go act the hero, every danger face / Love hates a coward's impotent embrace." Both publicly and privately, women confirmed this connection between bravery, manliness, and female admiration. "My only brother I have sent to the camp with my prayers and blessings," wrote a Philadelphia woman to a British officer in Boston. "I hope he will not disgrace me; I am confident he will behave with honour and emulate the great examples he has before him." A New Jersey woman was reported to have sent her husband off with a militant reminder: "Remember to do your duty! I would rather hear that you were left a corpse on the field than that you had played the part of a coward." A writer to the *Pennsylvania Evening Post,* calling herself a grandmother from New Jersey, spoke in similar martial tones, sending her sons and grandsons off with this request: "My children, I have a few words to say to you, you are going out in a just cause, to fight for the rights and liberties of your country; Let me beg of you . . . that if you fall, it may be like men."[7]

Whether women sent their men off with tears or praise, many of them experienced a devastating sense of loneliness after their husbands and sons departed. Lucy Knox, wife of Washington's leading artillery expert, General Henry Knox, was in no immediate danger while her husband served his country. Yet after filling her days with visits to friends, she found her evenings unbearable: "When I return home . . . [I] find myself entirely alone, to reflect that the only friend I have in the world is such an immense distance from me. . . ." The loneliness and anxiety felt by women whose husbands, sons, and lovers had enlisted was captured in a popular song:

> *Here I sit on Buttermilk Hill*
> *Who can blame me, cry my fill?*
> *And every tear would turn a mill,*
> *Since Johnny has gone for a soldier.*[8]

While men faced the enemy, women faced the challenge of managing on their own. With small children to tend, with prices quickly spiraling upward, with shortages of everyday necessities such as pins and medicines, and above all with the loss of the family members who normally tilled the fields, ran the shops, or worked the docks, women did their best to ensure that there would

41

be something to come home to when the soldiers came home.

Women everywhere improvised when household materials ran out. In rural South Carolina, women used thorns for pins. In other regions, they made tea from herbs and flowers. Lacking salt, they preserved foods with a concoction made of walnut ash. Resourceful and inventive women shared their secrets: a Providence, Rhode Island, woman found a way to improve the quality of homemade soap and published the recipe in the newspapers. "Take eight quarts of common family soap," she wrote, "and put to it about half a pint of common sea salt; boil this for a few minutes, then set it by and let it cool." The result, she promised, would be almost as good as the British soap urban women had become accustomed to buying.[9]

But not everything could be so easily replaced, and women were desperate for any existing stockpile of supplies. Even the rumor that a merchant was hoarding goods or asking exorbitant prices could provoke some women to radical actions. In 1778, Abigail Adams recorded an incident in Massachusetts:

> An eminent, wealthy, stingy merchant (also a bachelor) had a hogshead of coffee in his store, which he refused to sell . . . under six shillings per Pound. A number of Females, some say a hundred, some say more, assembled with a cart and trunks,

marched down to the Whare House and demanded the keys which he refused to deliver. Upon which one of them seizd him by his Neck and tossed him into the cart. Upon his finding no quarter, he delivered the keys when they tipped up the cart and discharged him; then opened the Warehouse, hoisted out the Coffee themselves, put it into the trunks and drove off. . . . A large concourse of men stood amazed silent Spectators.

News that a Connecticut merchant was holding back a supply of sugar, allegedly for the use of the army, prompted a similar raid upon his warehouse. According to the *Connecticut Courant* this was no haphazard, spontaneous event, but a well-organized, pseudomilitary maneuver. "A corps of female infantry, of 20 rank and file, with a flank of three chosen spirits of the male line," reported the newspaper, "march[ed] westward about one mile, in martial array and excellent order" and carried away the sugar "without any opposition from power, law, or conscience."[10]

But what "power, law, or conscience" could not prevent, spiraling inflation could. Inflation meant that women often lacked the funds to purchase goods even when they were available. "It's hard and cruel times to live," began one lament published in Marblehead, Massachusetts, "Takes thirty dollars to buy a sieve. / For money is not worth a pin, /

Had we but salt we've any thing, / For salt is all the Farmer's cry, / If we've no salt we sure must die." For poorer women, and especially for the wives of common soldiers, who were poorly paid when they were paid at all, this lament was no exaggeration. By 1778, four months of a soldier's pay could not purchase a barrel of wheat in many areas of the country. Fearing that they "sure must die," poorer women pleaded with their husbands to come home. "I am without bread," wrote one desperate soldier's wife, "the Committee will not supply me, my children will starve, or if they do not, they must freeze, we have no wood, neither can we get any—Pray Come Home." Widows of soldiers and seamen, cut off from even the meager wages their husbands had managed to send home, were in equally serious plights. After Mary Donnelly's husband was lost at sea, she was destitute. She dreaded waking each morning, she wrote, for she was "afraid to open my Eyes on the Daylight least I should hear my infant cry for Bread and not have it in my power to relieve him."[11]

Women in less desperate straits than Mary Donnelly could be overwhelmed as they tried to juggle their more difficult domestic chores with their new responsibilities in the fields. Although American farmwives were not total strangers to fieldwork, few had ever performed all the day-to-day tasks of this male sphere. Many tasks were both formidable and unfamiliar: fences to mend, firewood to cut and store, tools to repair—all this while there were babies to feed, children to watch, meals to cook, gardens to weed, and clothes to sew. Even if their task was to supervise those who performed the labor, the work was both new and demanding. Wives who had never negotiated the sale of crops, purchased farm equipment or supplies, paid laborers or bought and sold slaves, were now called upon to quickly develop these skills. For some, the result was a demystification of their husbands' gendered work roles; for many, the new duties brought a sense of pride in ownership that had never extended outside the home and garden. "Your farm" slowly became "our farm," in the letters of one wife to her absent husband; eventually, it became "my farm"—a shift in more than simple pronouns. A Connecticut woman put the transformation succinctly: "What was done," said Azubah Norton, with steely pride, "was done by myself." But even for the most successful of these surrogate husbands, the cost was high. Abigail Adams could write to John that she hoped "in time to have the Reputation of being as good a Farmeress as my partner has of being a Statesman." Yet she conceded "[I] hardly know how I have got thro these things but it gives me great pleasure to say that they are done because I know it will be an Ease to your mind."[12]

Women's efforts to save the family resources were made more difficult by the demands of the military. Whether they were victorious armies or armies on the run, they could destroy in a moment what women of all social classes had labored to preserve.

45

Women were asked, or ordered, by British, patriot, and loyalist commanders alike to bivouac soldiers on their property and officers in their homes. Parlors and kitchens were taken over, and the "hostess" was expected to provide food and do laundry for the military men who had commandeered their houses. These occupying troops drained more than a woman's energies; they depleted much-needed resources. Farm fences were destroyed, furniture burned, and storerooms emptied. Departing redcoat and Continental officers often ordered a woman's livestock slaughtered for the march ahead, drained her farm's supply of grain, and reaped the harvest of her gardens. In the south, departing British armies took plantation slaves with them, stripping women of their labor force and dividing slave families as well.[13]

Military officers might justify the taking of cattle, grain, and other supplies in support of their troops, but they had little excuse for the looting and malicious destruction that often accompanied their soldiers' arrival and departure. Abigail Adams wrote to her husband that Redcoats "burnt, broke, or hove into the water" everything they could not manage to take on board the transports that evacuated the British army from Boston. Wealthy women in Newport, Rhode Island, reported rings torn off their fingers, silver buckles ripped from their shoes, and their homes ransacked by British soldiers who occupied the town. A New Jersey woman, recovering from childbirth, had the cloak she wore over her shoulders torn away by a British soldier. When she challenged him, he swore that "if the Dam'd Rebel Bitch said a word more he Would run his bayonet threw her heart." Then he and his fellow soldiers "Plundered the House of Most of the Valuable goods." Still not satisfied, the men drew their bayonets and stabbed the bed in which the terrified woman lay, "until they Spoilt the Bed." In South Carolina, Eliza Lucas Pinckney, the daughter of one prosperous plantation owner and the wife of another, was only one of the southerners who watched her property and the property of her friends and neighbors destroyed. "The plantations," she wrote, "have been some quite, some nearly ruined and all with very few exceptions great sufferers. . . . Their Crops, Stock, boats, Carts, etc. all gone taken or destroyed and the Crops made this year will be very small by the desertion of the Negroes in planting and hoeing time."[14]

The loss of feather beds and parlor curtains, cattle and cloaks was often accompanied by damage to a woman's sense of propriety and dignity. The presence in her home of strangers, freely cursing and drinking, rattled the composure of many a colonial matron. But even more painful was the fear that soldiers evoked in the children of an occupied house. Elizabeth Drinker, a wealthy Quaker matron of Philadelphia, was furious when a British officer took over her house and moved in with "3 Horses 2 Cows 2 Sheep and 2 Turkeys . . . 3 Servants 2 White Men and one Negro Boy," but her deepest anger came when a drunken soldier terrified her children by brandishing his sword and swearing loudly inside her house.[15]

Perhaps the most vivid, and chilling, account of looting, came from Eliza Wilkinson, whose worst fears of the invasion by British and loyalist troops proved all too real. Helpless to prevent the soldiers from entering her home, she pleaded with "the inhumane monster who had my clothes . . . and begged him to spare me only a suit or two; but I got nothing but a curse for my pains; nay, so far was his callous heart from relenting, that, casting his eyes toward my shoes: 'I want them buckles,' said he." Wilkinson's nightmare was not over, however. Looters returned to her home, taking what they wanted and destroying what they did not need. "We have been humbled to the dust," she wrote, "again plundered, worse than ever plundered! Our very doors and window shutters were taken from the house, and carried aboard the vessels which lay in the river opposite our habitation; the sashes beaten out; furniture demolished; goods carried off; beds ripped up; stock of every kind driven away; in short, distresses of every nature attended us."[16]

Writing of her despair and depression, Eliza Wilkinson captured the feelings of many women, left alone to face the brutality and violence of the war. "The whole world appeared to me as a theatre, where nothing was acted but cruelty, bloodshed, and oppression; where neither age nor sex escaped the horrors of injustice and violence;

where lives and property of the innocent and inoffensive were in continual danger, and the lawless power ranged at large."[17]

Not all those who brought the "horrors of injustice and violence" were men. In some cases, women were also aggressors, driven as much by a desire for revenge as by political commitment. In the southern backcountry where a civil war raged between loyalist and patriot forces, women sometimes joined the marauders. When bands of roving, and sometimes rogue, loyalist soldiers swept through frontier settlements, loyalist women could be seen among them, dressed in clothing stolen from patriot homes and riding sidesaddle on stolen horses. During Britain's second southern campaign, the black women camp followers who trailed behind Cornwallis's army also engaged in looting. One British soldier marveled as these women picked a plantation or a town clean, like a "swarm of locusts." And in Poughkeepsie, New York, where several local loyalists were arrested for looting patriot homes, their number included five women, "three of whom are a mother and two daughters."[18]

Flight may have been the most sensible option for women when invading armies arrived. But where could they find safety? An upstate New Yorker spoke for many women when she wrote: "Where God can we fly from danger? All places appear equally precarious." As the British general John Burgoyne's army approached her home in

Tomhanick, New York, the poet Ann Eliza Bleecker did decide to flee, taking her four-year-old daughter and her infant child with her. "What thought my houses, lands and goods are gone," wrote Bleecker. "My babes remain—these I can call my own!" Yet Bleecker could not escape the dangers of war. Hiding in the woods, she watched helplessly as her infant daughter Abella died in her arms, a victim of exposure and hunger rather than enemy bullets. It was better, many women decided, to stay where they lived and face the consequences whatever they might be. "If the two opposite Armys were to come here alternately ten times," a Pennsylvania woman was reported to declare, she "would stand by her Property until she should be kill'd. If she must be a Beggar, it should be where she is known."[19]

Women who refused to flee their homes sometimes hid in cellars, listening to the sounds of troops moving through their towns. Others hid their valuables in the well and then huddled in a bedroom or parlor with their children, hoping that the soldiers would continue marching by. The risks were high and more was at stake than property and personal possessions. Poorly trained or callous soldiers sometimes entered homes firing their weapons randomly at residents. One of their victims was Hannah Ogden Caldwell, the wife of a patriot clergyman, who was killed by a soldier entering the bedroom where she and her nine children had gathered. His shot tore open her chest and punctured her lung. Not all fatalities were the result of recklessness, however. Both patriot and British forces committed conscious acts of fierce brutality. Patriot troops slaughtered the wife and children of a leading Mingo Indian; British troops cut a woman to pieces in her bed, her infant child by her side. Pregnant settlers on the borderlands were mutilated, their wombs ripped out of their dying bodies.[20]

For some women, the decision to remain in or leave their homes was not theirs to make. The ouster of women and children was frequently preparation for, or aftermath to, a widespread looting spree. After seizing New York City, for example, the British began to remove residents of adjoining Long Island and loot their empty homes. In New Jersey, British troops found Captain Thomas Brown's home unprotected and immediately "robbed it of everything of value," drove his wife and youngest children out, and burnt his house, barn, and shop to the ground. Like Captain Brown, militiaman William Gipson of South Carolina returned home in 1777 to find that "his mother, a widow woman, was tied up and whipped by the Tories, her house burned, and property all destroyed."[21]

Sometimes the destruction of property and the removal of women from their homes were tactics to force information out of the victims or to intimidate absent male members of the family. Suspicion that a man or his wife might be spying for the enemy also inspired raids on homes. This was the case when an armed band of patriots attacked the home of Vermont landowner Justus Sherwood, looking for evidence that he was gathering intelligence for the Canadian governor. Sherwood was, in fact, working for the enemy, but the raiding party found no proof of his spy activities. Frustrated perhaps, the Americans proceeded to smash the Sherwoods' furniture and steal their clothing. A belief that women were hiding fugitives in their homes could also prompt a raid. Dangerous as it was, some women hid both soldiers fleeing from the enemy and military deserters in secret rooms and in cellars. In one instance, a resourceful matron disguised several wounded men by clothing them in dresses and passing them off as female visitors. Some put themselves and their homes at risk for needy soldiers of both armies. Margaret Morris, a Quaker from Burlington, New Jersey, gave food and care to both American and British soldiers, remaining defiantly neutral in the midst of what was not only a revolution but a civil war. In 1777, Morris wrote that her heart melted to see a group of deserters lying asleep on the floor of a neighbor's house. She empathized with the men's suffering, no matter what their uniform, she said, and she sympathized with the mothers of these "innocent-looking lads."[22]

Although few spoke of it, women knew that the presence of the military always meant the possibility of rape or physical humiliation. Shame prevented most women from admitting to assault, even in peacetime, for a sexual double standard applied. Although the blame ought rightly to fall on the man, one gentleman conceded, yet "We Despise these poor Innocent Sufferers in this Brutal Crime as long as they live." During wartime, he admitted, more "Unnatural Miscreants are sure of Getting off with Impunity" and thus the number of rapes increased dramatically. In war as in peace, a pervasive sense of shame prevented women from reporting the attacks to authorities, although an unwanted pregnancy or death from venereal disease sometimes provided evidence of the crime. When in 1777 Congress called for a report on rape, the committee conceded that few victims came forward. Rape victims, they said, see it "as a kind of reproach to have the facts related, and their names known." Yet both the British and the Americans were willing to accuse the other of sexual atrocities. Newspapers and letters carried graphic details of gang rapes and the rape of young girls. A loyalist account claimed that the daughters of Flora MacDonald, an outspoken South Carolina supporter of the Crown, were taken prisoner by patriots who put "their swords into their bosoms, split down their silk dresses and, taking them out into the yard, stripped them of all their clothing." The *Pennsylvania Evening Post,* a patriot newspaper, printed a far more dramatic account of rape by British soldiers in New Jersey. "Besides the sixteen women who had fled to the woods to avoid their brutality and were there seized and carried off," it said, "one man had the cruel mortification to have his wife and only daughter (a child of ten years of age) ravished. . . . [A]nother girl of thirteen years of age was taken from her father's house, carried to a barn about a mile, there ravished, and afterwards made use of by five more of these brutes." An officer in the Continental Army described the treachery of General Howe's men while they were quartered in a village two miles from Princeton. The men "Pretended to a Young Woman That they was Searching for Rebels, and had been Informed that some of them were Secreted in the Barn and desired her to go with them and Show them the most Secret Places there, and She (Knowing that no body was there) to convince them, Went to the Barn with them." Once there, a soldier "Laid hold on her Strangled her to Prevent her crying out while the other Villain Ravisht her, and when he had done, he Strangled her Again While the Other Brute Repeated the horrid crime Upon her again." In the mind of this American officer, the British were more savage than the Indians: "This is far Worse," he wrote, "then an Indian War for I Never heard nor read of their Ravishing of Women Notwithstanding their cruelty to their captives." In July 1779, the *New York Journal* reported the fate of another group of too trusting American women, in a nearby Connecticut town. Believing that enemy soldiers would behave honorably, the women did not flee when the troops arrived. Instead, this "crew of British miscreants . . . behaved with worse than savage cruelty." Few of the young women, the older women, or "even the Negroes" escaped being raped, "some in the presence of their husbands, and others by great numbers successively." The aim of many of these alleged attacks may have been to demoralize and humiliate husbands and fathers, but it was the women and girls who suffered directly from them.[23]

Women could not rely on military commanders to regulate or punish their men in cases of rape or abuse. Much depended upon the individual character of the officer in charge. The American general Nathanael Greene lectured his troops in New York City in 1776 against bathing nude in a local mill pond, behavior he believed gave "Insult and Wound to the Modesty of female Decency," but Lord Rawdon, a British officer stationed on Staten Island, greeted news of the rape of local women with amusement. "The fair nymphs of this isle are in wonderful tribulation," Rawdon wrote, "as the fresh meat our men have got here has made them as riotous as satyrs. A girl cannot step into the bushes to pluck a rose without running the most imminent risk of being ravished, and they are so little accustomed to these vigorous methods that they don't bear them with proper resignation, and of consequence we have the most entertaining courtsmartial every day." Apparently Rawdon found the colonists too provincial to realize that women were spoils of war. He praised one woman for her sophistication in "not complaining after 7 men raped her."[24]

That women were victims of rape and humiliation and that they could not prevent attacks on their property or themselves says as much about the nature of the war and the culture of the soldier as it does about the women. With husbands and fathers gone and with children to protect, women knew that resistance would have consequences for lives other than their own. There were occasions on which women did choose to meet violence with violence, however, especially if their children were in mortal danger. In the borderland settlements, where Indian alliances with the British led to raids and door-to-door fighting, women armed themselves with what they could and fought back. In 1779, an account circulated of a Pittsburgh matron, Experience Bozarth, who split open one Indian attacker's head with an axe and then dealt a deadly blow to the body of a second assailant. Yet it was more common for women to defy the enemy by destroying their own property to prevent its use by the military. Thus, in upstate New York, Catherine Schuyler, wife of the American general Philip Schuyler, tossed flaming torches on her fields of wheat rather than see it used to feed General John Burgoyne's invading army. And as British occupying forces entered New York City in 1776, a woman was among those who chose to set the city ablaze rather than see it left intact for the enemy. Hearing the news of what became known as New York's Great Fire, Edmund Burke rose on the floor of the House of Commons to remind the British military of America's determination to be independent. "One miserable woman . . . with her single arm," Burke declared, had "arrested your progress, in the moment of your success. This miserable being was found in a cellar, with her visage besmeared and smutted over, with every mark of rage, despair, resolution, and the most exalted heroism, buried in combustibles, in order to fire New-York, and perish in its ashes."[25]

By war's end, tales of women who had defended their homes, destroyed property in order to deprive the enemy of its use, harbored fugitives, killed or wounded invaders, captured soldiers through trickery, or joined their men in protecting a home or a fort from enemy attack had begun to circulate. Exaggerated or true, these tales tell us as much about the desperate choices women faced in a home-front war as they do about the bravery or rashness that led them to resist.

For most women, the struggle to survive and to protect their children and their homes was challenge enough. Yet, they were pressed, and they pressed themselves, to do more—and there was much more to be done. General Washington's Continental troops were woefully short of everything from ammunition to clothing. State regiments lacked necessary supplies as well. If the production of homespun had been a political gesture in the years before the Revolution, now it was a critical necessity. Only a few months after the battles of Lexington and Concord, a call went out in Philadelphia to "the SPINNERS of this city, the suburbs, and country" to return to cloth production. Wool and cotton would be distributed to every spinner who came to Market and Ninth streets with a letter of reference from a "respectable person in their neighborhood." The broadside, posted across the city, de-clared that this was a call to public service that could be answered by the humblest of women. "The most feeble effort to help to save the state from ruin, when it is all you can do, is . . . entitled to the same reward as they who, of their abundant abilities, have cast in much." Local leaders in Hartford, Connecticut, preferred to order rather than urge the women of their town to produce clothing for the troops. Their production quota for 1776 was 1,000 coats and vests and 1,600 shirts. In the South, patriot leaders appealed to women to plant crops that could feed the local armies.[26]

Most of the women who contributed to the "public defense" did not need to be coerced. In the midst of their private struggles, they found the time to aid their country's cause. If the army needed saltpeter, women made saltpeter, boiling together wood ash and earth scraped from beneath the floors of their houses, adding charcoal and sulfur to produce the powder. If the army needed clothing, women like Mary Fraier of Chester

County, Pennsylvania, went door-to-door, soliciting clothes from their neighbors, then cleaned and mended them before delivering them to nearby troops. When the word spread that the military needed metal to produce bullets and cannon shot, women melted down their own pewter tableware, clock weights, and window weights, and solicited their neighbors to do the same. One New Englander even donated the name plaques from her family's tombstones.

And everywhere that the battlefield yielded its wounded, women volunteered to provide beds and care for the soldiers. Sick as well as wounded soldiers found doors opened to them as women willingly housed soldiers inoculated for smallpox— and then welcomed these same young men back into their homes if the disease took hold. "I was ordered back to Widow Dimond's, with whom I was quartered when inoculated," recalled Samuel Larrabee of Maine, and she "nursed me and got me well." Few sites seemed too dangerous for women like Elizabeth Burgin, who brought baskets of food and supplies to the captured American soldiers held aboard the notorious floating prison ships in New York Harbor.[27]

Philadelphia's humblest women answered the call to aid the war effort with their spinning wheels in the early years of the war; the city's elite women organized their own public campaign in 1780. The American victory at Saratoga and the signing of the treaty of alliance with France had lifted the spirits and raised the morale of the urban upper classes. Suddenly confident that America would win its war for independence, prosperous families engaged in a frenzy of spending and socializing. But the costly balls and parties, the elegant new clothing and elaborately dressed hair did not sit well with several of Philadelphia's most distinguished matrons, among them the wife of the governor, Esther DeBerdt Reed, and the daughter of Benjamin Franklin, Sarah Franklin Bache. Reed and Bache thought it shameful that Washington's soldiers were suffering from shortages of rations, clothing, and supplies while their own friends and neighbors threw away money on luxuries. Disturbed that republican virtue was being sacrificed to excess and self-indulgence, the two women organized the Ladies Association and launched the biggest domestic fund-raising campaign of the war. The campaign began on June 12 with the publication of Reed's "Sentiments of an American Woman," a call to sacrifice, a life of simplicity, and a return to "the same sentiments which animated us at the beginning of the Revolution."[28]

In "Sentiments," Reed provided one of the most sustained justifications for women's active role in public service. Women could not be content, she argued, with mere expressions of sympathy for the Revolutionary cause. Instead, they must be truly useful. Reed recognized that social norms, especially within her own genteel class, forbade women "march[ing] to glory by the same paths as the

Men." But women could show, and had shown in the past, courage, constancy, and patriotism. She cited a long list of historical heroines who were "Born for Liberty"—naming biblical figures such as Deborah and Queen Esther and, later, saints such as Joan of Arc, but also including all the anonymous women who in wartime had ignored "the weakness of their sex" and built fortifications, dug trenches with their bare hands, and sacrificed their jewels, fine clothing, and money to save their country. With their own country in danger, she called on American women to make similar sacrifices for the sake of the common soldiers who had secured Philadelphia's current tranquillity at great risk to their own lives. "Let us be engaged to offer the homage of our gratitude at the altar of military valor," she wrote, and, then, in an addendum, Reed and Sarah Franklin Bache laid out their remarkable fund-raising plan.[29]

The Ladies Association plan was both ambitious and efficient. It called for every woman and girl in the state of Pennsylvania to come forward with whatever "patriotic offering" she felt she could afford. No contribution, however small, would be rejected. "The shilling offered by the Widow or the young girl," wrote Reed and Bache, "will be received as well as the most considerable sums presented by the Women who have . . . greater means." To speed the collection process, the women of each county would elect a "Treasuress" to receive the contributions and record each donation in her register. Only contributions in the amount of twenty dollars would be accepted by this treasuress; thus women who could not afford that much were encouraged to pool their resources in order to produce the required amount. One woman from each of the pooling groups would be responsible for delivering the money to the treasuress and for signing the register to confirm the group contribution. The treasuress would then send the register and the money to the wife of the governor of the state, and she in turn would forward the money to "Mistress Washington." The final step was for Martha Washington to deliver the contributions to "the first Soldier of the Republic," General George Washington.[30]

On the day after "Sentiments" appeared in the local newspaper, the Ladies Association met and divided the city of Philadelphia into ten districts. Several days later, the *Maryland Gazette* carried a letter from one of the participants to a friend in Annapolis, describing the contagious enthusiasm for the project among Philadelphia women. Forty women were needed to canvass, she wrote, and forty women volunteered, among them a new mother so eager to participate that she arranged to have her baby nursed by a friend while she made her rounds. The women were remarkably thorough, but, she added, they were also remarkably tactful: they attempted to pass over the homes of women known to be indigent or without funds to spare. Yet even the poorest residents asked to be included.

When the canvassers failed to knock on the door of an elderly woman "in circumstances not easy," she "came with tears in her eyes to present her offering." The campaign served not only to show appreciation to the soldiers, but also to allow former loyalists or women lukewarm in their devotion to the Revolution an opportunity to make amends. The campaign even benefited from romance. "Several bachelors," the anonymous letter writer continued, "begged to have the honour of subscribing, thinking it the best means to recommend themselves to their favourite ladies."[31]

Bachelors were not the only men to applaud the radical sight of genteel women taking to the streets, knocking on the doors of strangers, and soliciting funds. No less a figure than the Marquis de Lafayette sent a donation to the campaign on behalf, he explained, of his own wife. The French minister, Marquis de la Luzerne, followed suit, making a donation in honor of his wife. Philadelphia's most prominent men were equally enthusiastic. Benjamin Rush, husband of association member Julia Stockton Rush, wrote with pride to John Adams: "My dear wife, who you know in the beginning of the war had all the timidity of her sex as to the issue of the war and the fate of her husband, was one of the ladies employed to solicit benefactions for the army. She distinguished herself by her zeal and address in this business, and is now so thoroughly enlisted in the cause of her country that she reproaches me with lukewarmness."[32]

Not everyone approved, of course. Anna Rawle, a Philadelphia loyalist, criticized the campaign. Disgusted by the sight of "a number of very genteel women, parad[ing] about the streets," Rawle described what she considered to be little more than an extortion effort in a long letter to her mother that June. "But of all absurdities the Ladies going about for money exceeded everything; they were so extremely importunate that people were obliged to give them something to get rid of them. . . ."[33]

Twenty years earlier, the public activities of the Ladies Association would surely have been condemned in terms even stronger than Rawle's. But in 1780, in the midst of the war, elite women in other states did not hesitate to emulate Esther Reed and her band of fund-raisers. The association leaders did all they could to see the movement spread, reaching out through a social network to family, friends, and acquaintances in rural Pennsylvania, in Virginia, and in Maryland. In Maryland, no less prominent a figure than Mary Digges Lee, the wife of Governor Thomas Sim Lee, led her state's fund-raising campaign. Martha Washington promoted the campaign in Virginia, writing to Martha Wayles Jefferson to ask her to establish a Ladies Association there. Although the ailing wife of Thomas Jefferson was unable to join the campaign, she forwarded the appeal to Eleanor Madison, the wife of the president of the College of William and Mary, and the mother of James Madison. Thomas Jefferson, who was well known for his opposition to women's participation in, or concern with, politics, would have been shocked by his wife's views on the campaign. "I undertake with chearfulness," she said in her letter to Eleanor Madison, "the duty of furnishing to my countrywomen an opportunity of proving that they also participate of those virtuous feelings of patriotism."[34]

Before the year ended, New Jersey and Maryland women had collected almost $32,000 in paper money. Virginia's association groups boasted collections ranging from $1,560 to $7,506, no small feat in a state with few towns and many isolated farms and plantations. Reed and Bache's original Philadelphia campaign brought in more than $300,000 in paper currency, donated by over 1,600 people. The women assumed that they had the right to determine how and on whom the thousands of dollars they had collected would be spent. Reed and Bache had been quite specific in their plan. They did not mean to relieve the government of its obligation to feed and clothe its soldiers; their "extraordinary bounty [was] intended to render the condition of the Soldier more pleasant." Reed believed the money should go directly to the soldiers, to do with as they saw fit. Yet Washington believed he knew better how the money should be employed: on shirts for the soldiers. Writing to Esther Reed on August 10, 1780, Washington attempted to present his decision in the best light.

"It was not my intention to divert the benevolent donation of the Ladies from the channel they wished it to flow in," he began. Yet he felt certain that the distribution of cash to his men would have bad consequences. "A few provident Soldiers will, probably, avail themselves of the advantages which may result from the generous bounty of two dollars in Specie, but it is equally probable that it will be the means of bringing punishment on a number of others whose [propensity] to drink overcoming all other considerations too frequently leads them into irregularities and disorders." The much-needed shirt, he concluded, would be a wiser choice.[35]

In the end, the women bowed to the pressure from Washington. By September 1780 Sarah Bache would report to her father, Benjamin Franklin, that she was "busily imploy'd in cutting out and making shirts, and giving them out to make to the good women of my acquaintance, for our Brave Soldiers." Rather than use up any of the valuable contributions they had gathered to pay others to make the shirts, the Ladies Association members had taken on the chore themselves.[36]

Esther DeBerdt Reed did not live to see the dispersal of the shirts she and other members of her Ladies Association completed. On September 27, two days after she died of acute dysentery, the *Pennsylvania Gazette* carried her obituary, citing her patriotism and her contributions to the cause of independence. "Those disposed to lessen the

66

reputation of female patriotism might have said that what our women have contributed, must, in the first instance, have come from the pockets of their husbands; but, where their own labour is bestowed, the most delicate fingers being employed in the workmanship, it must be acknowledged an effort of virtue, the praise of which must peculiarly belong to themselves." In the end, it was that most mundane of women's domestic chores—sewing—that Reed's city of Philadelphia chose to honor.[37]

CHAPTER 4

"SUCH A SORDID SET OF CREATURES IN HUMAN FIGURE"

Women Who Followed the Army

In October 1777, American troops managed a minor miracle: the defeat of General John Burgoyne's army at Saratoga, New York. The American victory stunned the British, delighted the French, and persuaded many Americans that independence just might be attainable. Under the terms of the surrender, over five thousand soldiers and officers were to be marched to Boston and shipped back to England, bound by a promise never to serve again in the war against America. As the defeated British and Hessian troops trudged through Boston, Hannah Winthrop watched the spectacle with sympathetic horror. Moving by her in great number were "poor, dirty, emaciated men," part of a once great and confident army that had found itself lost, near starvation, and badly beaten by an upstart force of volunteers and self-taught officers. But trailing behind these soldiers, Winthrop also saw "great numbers of women, who seemed to be the beasts of burthen, having a bushel basket on their back, by which they were bent double." These baskets did not hold military supplies; instead they seemed to be filled with "Pots and Kettles, various sorts of Furniture, children peeping through . . . and other utensils," and finally, "some very young infants who were born on the road." The women Winthrop saw were barefoot and dressed in rags. As they passed, the stink of long hours of exertion and long abandoned hygiene produced an "effluvia [that] filled the air." "I never had the least Idea," Winthrop wrote, "that the Creation produced such a sordid set of creatures in human Figure."[1]

Like Winthrop, militia private Daniel Granger had been struck by the sad circumstances of the almost two thousand women who brought up the rear of the march. Despite the chill in the October air, the women wore "short Petty coats" and were "bare footed & bare Leged." As they walked, they were slowed by the huge packs they carried on their backs and by the children they carried in their arms. An air of resignation surrounded them, Granger added, and "they were silent, civil, and looked quite subdued."[2]

If Winthrop and Granger were touched by the condition of these women, neither of them was surprised by females traveling with the army. American civilians called these women camp followers. The British called them "trulls" or "doxies." Quartermasters and supply officers listed them in their records as living pieces of "baggage." Generals called them necessary nuisances. Yet there was a grudging recognition on the part of everyone that these women had a place in the British and American army camps and forts and even in the heat of battle: as cooks, washerwomen, seamstresses, nurses, scavengers for supplies, sexual partners, and occasionally as soldiers and spies.

No one knows how many "nuisances" there were—whether they numbered in the thousands or tens of thousands. The numbers rose and fell by the seasons, expanding during the winter months when the armies were stationary, decreasing when the fighting was renewed. In the American army, the female population varied widely from unit to unit; units formed in an area hard hit by the war or occupied by the enemy always attracted more women than units formed in safer regions. Not surprisingly, historians' estimates of the number of women with the American army vary widely, from a claim that twenty thousand women marched with the American military to a more conservative estimate that women made up roughly 3 percent of the population in army camps.

Perhaps five thousand women, and a remarkable twelve thousand children, experienced life in a British military camp before the war ended. The British transport ships arrived with some women aboard, usually the wives of noncommissioned officers, but the majority of the women who followed the British armies came from American cities and farms. Because the British were better equipped and supplied, they attracted more camp followers than the poorly provisioned Continental Army. Since five of every six British soldiers were single, they welcomed these women as temporary "camp wives." Most of these camp marriages ended when the British returned home. But many of the five thousand Hessian mercenaries who deserted their regiments and settled in America began their new lives with the American women who had been their camp wives.[3]

What drove most of these thousands of women to join the armies was simple enough: loneliness, poverty, fear of starvation, the possibility of rape or death at the hands of hostile invading troops. The army was the court of last resort for wives, widows, runaway servants, and any woman who faced poverty because of the war. The military rations they received might be small and the conditions in the camps dismal, but meager meals and shared tents were preferable to no food or shelter at all. In an ironic sense, becoming a camp follower was an act of independent decision making, a choice that carried many women hundreds of miles away from their homes and friends. Yet if life in the camps meant survival, it did not mean personal liberation. Military culture reinforced female dependency; it was intensely hierarchical and the chain of command was entirely male. Civilian women may have expected to serve as helpmates to their husbands or fathers, but camp followers could be called on to provide housewifely services like cooking, sewing, and washing to literally hundreds of men. Camp followers did resist stringent rules and regulations and excessive workloads and meager pay, but these expressions of autonomy always carried the threat of punishment—or banishment. Women drummed out of the camp were sobering examples for those who remained.

Not all the women in military camps were refugees from civilian life, of course. Sutlers and tradeswomen came to the army camps to ply their wares, and prostitutes came to ply theirs. The wives of generals and colonels came to lift the morale of their officer husbands, to organize as gala a social season of dances and dinners as was possible in the winter encampments, and then to return home when spring brought a new military campaign. But the majority of camp followers were women who came from the lower ranks of society, and the same class distinctions that separated the common soldiers from their officers carried over to the soldiers' companions as well.

While officers may have embraced the newer, more romantic notions of delicacy and refinement among women of their own class, their respect did not extend to the poorer camp followers, who seemed oblivious to every rule of feminine behavior. Camp followers cursed and drank like men, preferred to steal rather than to starve, and appeared in public when they were pregnant. To many officers, they had forfeited all claim to respect or chivalry. As one American officer put it, these women were "the ugliest in the world to be collected . . . the furies who inhabit the infernal Regions can never be painted half so hideous as these women."

Even unmarried enlisted men spoke disparagingly of the women who traveled with their regiments. Watching the women bring up the rear on a march in 1780, Private Joseph Plumb Martin wrote, "It was truly amusing to see [their] number and habilments . . . of all specimens of human beings, this group capped the whole. A caravan of wild beasts could bear no comparison with it. There was 'Tag, Rag and Bobtail'; 'some in rags and some in jags,'" he added, making sarcastic reference to the lines of a popular tune, "but none 'in velvet gowns.' Some with 2 eyes, some with one, and some I believe with none at all." Martin's obvious relish at the sight of these ragged and deformed women may have been little more than regional pride (or provinciality), for he was a proud New Englander and they were following regiments from the middle states. But his harsh judgment that they were "odd and disgusting" was not an uncommon one.[4]

No camp followers of Martin's own Connecticut regiment wore "velvet gowns," of course. Women who flocked to the armies, or came across the ocean with them, did so precisely because they were needy. A typical British soldier's wife might arrive with little more than a gown or two, a cloak, a petticoat, a few aprons, a pair of shoes, and perhaps a blanket and some clothing for their children. After months of marching with the army, sleeping in fields or in crowded huts, carrying pots, pans, and children on their backs or in their arms, both the women and their clothing began to grow ragged. When their clothing wore thin, camp followers willingly donned the coats or shirts they removed from dead or dying soldiers, thus adding to their "odd and disgusting" appearance. They had few other choices, for neither military nor civilian governments considered clothing women and children to be their responsibility. When Governor Joseph Reed of Pennsylvania made the novel recommendation that the women of the Pennsylvania regiments be given "a new gown, silk handkerchief, and a pair of shoes," the state legislature refused.

Perhaps the sight of several women marching with Burgoyne's army through a heavy snowstorm with little more to cover them than an "old oil-cloth" prompted Thomas Anburey to conclude that "the women who follow a camp are of such a masculine nature, they are able to bear all hardships."[5] But these women did not arrive in camp more masculine in nature than the women who remained at home. Military life had hardened them. Eager to provide food for their children and for themselves, women often plundered and looted as their army traveled through the countryside. A British soldier described them as a "swarm of beings—no better than harpies" and British officers worried that their plundering turned local citizens into bitter enemies of the king. During battle, women could be seen moving among the fallen bodies, "expos[ing] themselves," as Connecticut soldier Ambrose Collins recorded, "where the shots were flying, to strip the dead." It was not their bravery under fire that he remembered, however; watching them move from body to body he could only conclude that they were "doubtless the basest of their sex." But if the brutality of warfare had made these women callous, or inured them to suffering and death, it had apparently done the same to him. "I saw one woman while thus employed," he wrote with little sympathy, "struck by a cannon ball and literally dashed to pieces."[6]

George Washington was especially perplexed and annoyed by the women who sought refuge in his camps. For although camp-following was a long-standing tradition within the British army, the American commanders had little experience with the presence of women among the military. Their colonies had relied on militias, locally based and called out—usually for brief service—only during crises. In August 1777, the general complained: "The multitude of women in particular, especially those who are pregnant, or have children are a clog upon every movement."[7] Perhaps even worse, the women refused to obey Washington's instructions. Before the war was

75

over, the general had issued eight armywide orders directing women to march with the baggage and prohibiting them from riding on the baggage wagons. Yet his officers had little success in ensuring that these directions were followed.

Not even Washington himself could make the camp followers obey. When the Continental Army marched through Philadelphia after the British abandoned the city, Washington ordered the women and children to travel on the side streets, or with the baggage in the rear, or, if possible, outside the city entirely. But, as one Philadelphia observer pointed out, the orders fell on deaf ears. The women were "spirited off into the quaint, dirty little alleyways and side streets. But they hated it. The army had barely passed through the main thoroughfares before these camp followers poured after their soldiers again, their hair flying, their brows beady with the heat, their belongings slung over one shoulder, chattering and yelling in sluttish shrills as they went and spitting in the gutters."[8] The contrast between Esther Reed's genteel volunteers, moving through those same streets on their fundraising mission, and these women, bred in poverty or sunk into it because of the war, was implicit.

A frustrated Washington had recommended to his officers "to use every reasonable method . . . to get rid of all such as are not absolutely necessary." Yet, as even Washington would have had to admit, most of the women *were* "absolutely necessary," if for no other reason than to cut down on desertions. A harsh policy, the general conceded, would mean he would "lose by Desertion, perhaps to the Enemy, some of the oldest and best soldiers in the Service." The men needed the comfort of their wives, or their mothers, especially when they were sick or wounded. "Will you not send for my mother?" pleaded one ailing soldier. "If she were here to nurse me I could get well."[9]

But there were other reasons besides morale to keep women in the camps. One of them was hygiene. Dirty uniforms were a pressing problem in every regiment, yet men accustomed to their mothers, sisters, or wives doing the laundry balked at performing this traditionally female chore. To accommodate their troops, American and British armies required camp followers to serve as washerwomen for both officers and enlisted men. Regiments like New York's 2nd and 3rd calculated the ratio of washerwomen to soldiers that was "absolutely necessary": for 248 men, the 2nd regiment required two women; the 3rd, with 435 men, listed their needs at four women, or one washerwoman for every 109 men. Maryland camp followers escaped such remarkable workloads, for their regiments set the ratio at one woman for every 24 men, or, more humanely, one for every 10.[10]

Both armies required the men to pay the women for their services, although wages were generally meager. British washerwomen received three pence a week for shirts. At West Point, a June 1780 order by the American command addressed to "the Women, who draw provisions, with their respective Companies," listed the following prices: "For a Shirt, two Shillings; Woolen Breeches, Vest and Overalls, two Shillings, each; Linen Vest & Breeches, one Shilling, each; Linen Overalls, one Shilling & Six Pence, each; Stockings & Handkerchief, Six Pence, each; The Women who wash for the Companies will observe these regulations." Apparently some camp followers resented the low value placed on their skills. In 1778, the 2nd Pennsylvania Regiment felt it necessary to issue this directive: "Should any woman refuse to wash for a soldier at the above rate he must make complaint to the officers commanding the company to which he belongs . . . who [if they] find it proceeds from laziness or any other improper excuse" can dismiss the woman. Any guilty washerwoman who attempted to remain with her husband would be drummed out of the camp. Camp followers who did not resist their assignment did try to make their task easier whenever possible; a favorite shortcut was to do the laundry in the soldiers' drinking water.[11]

The demand for washerwomen was usually greater than the supply and officers often turned to women in neighboring towns or on nearby farms to do their laundry. Yet even captains and colonels found the cost of cleanliness a drain on their pocketbooks. Writing home to his brother from his camp near Morristown in January 1780, Colonel Ebenezer

Huntington complained about the impact of inflation: "Money is good for nothing . . . my Washing bill is beyond the limits of my Wages." The solution, Huntington concluded, was to "hire some Woman to live in Camp to do the Washing for myself and some of the Officers." His only hesitation was the gossip that might ensue about the nature of the woman's duties. "I am aware that many Persons will tell the Story to my disadvantage."[12]

The shortage of washerwomen meant more than dirty uniforms and unsavory-smelling underwear. In the crowded tents of an army camp, poor sanitation was a breeding ground for communicable diseases like typhus, dysentery, and respiratory illnesses. With far fewer camp followers than the British army, the American army was harder hit by these deadly diseases, as well as by lice and other debilitating infestations. And this meant a greater need for nurses. Washington and his officers recruited both within and outside the camps for women willing to serve as nurses. The risks were high since tending the sick meant exposure to the diseases. The work was unpleasant, the hours grueling, and the pay poor. The job description, issued by General Washington himself, did little to make the work appealing:

The NURSES, in the absence of the Mates [male attendants], administer the medicine and diet prescribed for the sick according to order, they obey all orders they receive from the Matron; not only to be attentive to the cleanliness of the wards and patients, but to keep themselves clean. They are never to be disguised with liquor; they are to see that the close-stools or pots are to be emptied as soon as possible after they are used . . . They are to see that every patient, upon his admission into the Hospital is immediately washed with warm water and that his face and hands are washed and head combed every morning . . . that their wards arc swcpt over every morning or oftener if necessary and sprinkled with vinegar three or four times a day. . . .

For their endless rounds of sweeping, emptying bedpans and chamber pots, bathing patients, and disinfecting the wards, nurses were to receive one ration and twenty-four cents per day—about 10 percent of what surgeons and male attendants made.[13]

As cooks, seamstresses, washerwomen, and nurses, camp followers engaged in traditional female roles in an untraditional setting. But army life frequently required, or evoked, bravery and daring usually associated with men. Joseph Plumb Martin, who had such a hostile attitude toward the middle states' camp followers, was nevertheless impressed by the courage under fire shown by a woman at Fort Monmouth. "A woman whose husband belonged to the artillery and who was then attached to a piece in the engagement," he wrote, "attended her husband at the piece the whole time. While in the act of reaching a cartridge and having one of her feet as far before the other as she could step, a cannon shot from the enemy passed directly between her legs without doing any other damage than carrying away all the lower part of her petticoat. Looking at it with apparent unconcern, she observed that it was lucky it did not pass a little higher, for in that case it might have carried away something else." Martin admired her wit, but the fact that she "continued her occupation" without pause earned his grudging respect. Soldiers at the battle of Brandywine hailed the women of Pennsylvania's 6th Regiment for their heroism. Although "frequently cautioned as to the danger of coming into the line of fire," these wives took "the empty canteens of their husbands and friends and returned with them filled with water . . . during the hottest part of the engagement." And hungry soldiers appreciated the determination of General Washington's cook, Sarah Osborn, who did not let the bombardment at Yorktown prevent her from cooking and carrying "beef, and bread, and coffee . . . to the soldiers in the entrenchments." Other soldiers admitted admiration for women's fortitude and stamina on the army's long marches through the countryside. When Sergeant Grier's wife, "a large virtuous and respectable woman" traveling with Benedict Arnold's disastrous expedition to Canada, lifted her skirt waist high and waded gingerly through a swamp, the soldier behind her declared "my mind was humbled, yet astonished at the exertions of this good woman."[14]

Women who crossed the gender line, posing as male soldiers, were greeted with more ambivalence. Often a woman's motivation seemed to make the difference between admiration and contempt. Women whose devotion to a man drove them to masquerade as soldiers were frequently admired, while women who seemed enticed by the enlistment bounty provoked the wrath of officers and enlisted men. A calculated deception was condemned more readily than a spontaneous crossing of gender lines. Finally, women whose sex was discovered quickly were more likely to be punished severely, while women who saw combat before their sex was revealed sometimes drew praise. Thus, men might praise the spontaneous action of a group of women who dressed as men to convince attackers that there were more defenders inside a fort than they had bargained for. They might applaud the devotion of a woman like Anna Maria Lane, who, when her husband enlisted in the Continental Army, donned men's clothing and enlisted with him. And they might be sympathetic to a tale of cruelly separated lovers, reunited only after the woman posed as a man, journeyed to America, and endured "such fatigue as scarce any of her sex could have undergone" before finding her wounded fiancé. The American government might even grant a pension to a woman like Margaret Corbin, who wore men's clothing as she stood beside her husband at Fort Washington, took his place in the heat of battle, and was wounded, captured, and came home a permanently disabled veteran of the war. But when military officials discovered that Ann Bailey had collected a bounty by posing as a man and enlisting under the name Samuel Gay, they discharged her, fined her, and put her in jail for two weeks. Anne Smith fared no better. On June 27, 1782, the *Massachusetts Spy* reported: "A person appearing in a publick house in this town and offering to serve in the continental army for the term of three years, was inlisted by the name of Samuel Smith. . . . After many enquiries and a very minute examination, this adventurer (although artfully dressed in man's apparel) was discovered to be of the female sex; and soon after conducted to gaol. . . ." Smith was condemned not only for attempting to collect an $80 enlistment bounty under the falsest of pretenses, but for almost evading discovery. "She acted the man so perfectly well through the whole," the newspaper reported, "that she might probably have passed, had not the want of a beard, and a redundance of some other matters led to a detection." Sometimes even an appeal to romance failed to move the male authorities. A young woman whose father would not let her marry the man she loved disguised herself and enlisted. The recruiters suspected the young recruit was actually a female. They forced her to undergo a physical examination and then ordered "the Drums to beat her threw the Town with the Whores march" while she was still dressed as a man. The legendary Deborah Sampson had better luck: she served undetected as Private Robert Shurtleff for several years, and, when her sex was discovered, the army honorably discharged her and the state of Massachusetts granted her a veteran's pension. Perhaps the most successful masquerader was Sally St. Clair, a woman of French and African background who managed to hide her sex from the army until her death at the siege of Savannah in 1782.[15]

Despite their usefulness and their acts of bravery, camp followers did present the military with a host of problems. Wives goaded husbands into fights with fellow soldiers or convinced them to desert the army; they sold rum and liquor illegally to the troops; they harassed and insulted "decent women" as they marched through town and countryside; they engaged in shouting matches with officers over provisions, rations, and sexual advances; they cheated on their husbands and stole from their friends. British commanders in Boston in 1775 were convinced that a smallpox epidemic among their men had been brought to their camps by women who ignored quarantine signs on houses they had targeted for looting. Women's infractions and crimes required the army to police them, try them, and determine the appropriate punishments. Often those punishments were severe. Mary Johnson was given a hundred lashes for trying to entice American soldiers at Valley Forge to desert, and Isabella MacMahan received the same number for knowingly receiving stolen goods. Women found guilty of theft or prostitution could be ducked under water, whipped, or drummed out of the camp. The unfortunate Winifred McCowan, a British camp follower in occupied Boston, was tried by court-martial "for having stolen [a] bull and causing him to be killed." Found guilty, McCowan was tied up, pulled behind a cart, and given a hundred lashes on her bare back "in different portion of the most public parts of the town and camp." She was then imprisoned for three months. The constant presence of women made the camps less secure, for both armies enlisted women to spy for them. Thus, innocent-seeming tradeswomen, plying sewing materials or food or liquor, might also be studying the military strength and numbers in the camp, eavesdropping on strategy planning sessions, or wangling information out of indiscreet soldiers.[16]

The presence of prostitutes was especially troubling to the more moral, or less sophisticated, American military leadership. During its brief tenure in New York City, Washington's army attracted an alarming number of prostitutes to its camp. The most notorious meeting ground for soldiers and prostitutes was a field owned by

St. Paul's church and thus known to its visitors as "Holy Ground." Holy Ground was not simply decadent; it was dangerous. Several limbs and heads of men were reportedly found there, victims, it was alleged, of murderous prostitutes. A colonel who patrolled Holy Ground to prevent or break up fights between prostitutes and soldiers described the women in the most damning terms: "bitchfoxy jades, jills, haggs, strums, prostitutes." He called his assignment "Hell's work." Another officer, whose curiosity brought him to Holy Ground, was appalled by the women he saw. "At first," he wrote, "I thought nothing could exceed them for impudence and immodesty; but I found the more I was acquainted with them the more they excelled in their Brutallity. To mention the Particulars of their Behavior would so pollute the Paper I write upon that I must excuse myself." Despite the obvious dangers, he admitted that many officers and men regularly frequented the site. When the British occupied New York in 1776, their soldiers proved just as willing to risk the dangers of Holy Ground. Here, and in Canvas Town, an area between Great Dock and Water Street, they patronized the prostitutes of the city.[17]

American soldiers camped in the countryside were less disturbed by the presence of "jills" and "strums" among them. In his diary, Massachusetts-born Benjamin Gilbert recorded the comings and goings of two prostitutes named Betsy and Marcy who regularly visited his tent. On April 28, 1778, he wrote: "At Nigt. Marcy was at our tent and lay all Nigt with Serjt Phipps and went home at gun firing in the morning." By May, however, Marcy had been arrested, along with another prostitute, Polly Robinson. And, on June 5, Gilbert recorded that Polly Robinson and another prostitute, Nel Tidrey, were "drummed out of the Regt."[18]

Both British and American commanders tried to regulate the presence of prostitutes, if not for moral reasons then because outbreaks of venereal disease would reduce the number of combat-ready soldiers. In the fall of 1778, a doctor with American troops at Fredericksburg, New York, reported twenty men hospitalized with venereal disease. The following summer, West Point doctors reported over thirty cases. Regimental commanders issued orders like one from a New York officer declaring that "No Woman of Ill Fame Shall be permitted to Come into the Barricks on pain of Being well Watred under a pump, and Every Officer or Soldier who Shall Bring in Any Such woman will be tried and Punished by a Court Martial." But, as the busy scene at Holy Ground demonstrated, army officials had little control over prostitutes who worked outside the camp or over the men who visited them. The diarist Benjamin Gilbert kept track of his fifteen outings to a brothel he called "Wyoma."[19]

Camp followers who were not prostitutes might nevertheless be carriers of venereal disease. In an effort to protect his soldiers but still show some respect for the modesty of the married women of the camp, the commander of a Delaware regiment ordered "that the Weoman belonging to the Regt. Be paraded tomorrow morning & to undergo an examination from the Surgeon of the Regiment at his tent except those that are married & the husbands of those to undergo said examination." Any woman refusing to be examined would be drummed out of the camp.[20]

The wives and mistresses of generals and other high-ranking officers were not subjected to such humiliating examinations, of course. They did not belong to the army in the same sense as the camp followers who received rations or payment for services and thus they were not subject to military regulation. American wives such as Catharine Greene, wife of Nathanael Greene, and the heavyset, no-nonsense Lucy Knox, wife of the equally portly Henry Knox, joined their officer husbands during the winter months, at encampments like Valley Forge or Morristown. None was more faithful than Martha Washington, who came every winter, making the long journey from Mount Vernon to Washington's camp outside Boston in 1775 and traveling to New York, Morristown, and Valley Forge as the war progressed. An aide to the Prussian General von Steuben declared that her arrival "inspired fortitude."[21]

Martha Washington visited the men in their tents at Valley Forge, but she did not share the hunger and cold with them. She, like Catharine Greene, took up winter quarters in nearby farmhouses. Doting husbands like General Greene always sought the best accommodations for their wives. When Greene's "Caty" arrived at Valley Forge, she was escorted to a residence far more elegant than that of the commander in chief himself. Many of the women arrived with servants or slaves in tow, but, if more assistance was needed, the officers assigned enlisted men and African American slaves to their staffs.

The arrival of Martha Washington or Caty Greene marked the beginning of a makeshift social season for the officers, who viewed the generals' wives as charming diversions from the depressing realities of war. As General Greene wrote to a friend in March 1779: "We had a little dance at my head-quarters. . . . Upon the whole we had a pretty little frisk." The generals' wives organized balls and dinner parties and engaged in furious rounds of matchmaking. Alexander Hamilton met his future wife, Elizabeth Schuyler, at one of these social events. Despite the gaiety, the impact of wartime shortages and limited resources was noticeable; at one officers' party, no one could be admitted unless he wore "a whole pair of breeches."[22]

The wives of British generals rarely made the transatlantic journey, although the wife of the Hessian commander, Baron von Riedesel, traveled to Quebec with three small children to join her husband. Unaccompanied generals usually acquired local camp wives or mistresses, occasionally with the approval of the women's husbands. General William Howe, for example, enjoyed the company of Elizabeth Loring for three years, apparently with the blessings of Joshua Loring, who, perhaps not coincidentally, was appointed commissary general of prisoners. Howe's relationship with this hard-drinking, gambling woman popularly known as "the Sultana" became the subject of poem and song. When a New Jersey congressman, Francis Hopkinson, composed a ballad in praise of a new American explosive device, much of the poem was devoted to the Howe-Loring affair. "Sir William he, snug as a flea," one stanza began, "Lay all the time a snoring; / Nor dreamed of harm as he lay warm / in bed with Mrs. L——g." Baroness von Riedesel was shocked to discover that most of the "cousins" of British generals introduced to her at headquarters in Quebec were not cousins at all. "I learned afterwards, that every one of these gentlemen had the same kind of cousins residing with them . . . who in order to avoid scandal, were forced almost every year to absent themselves for a little while, on account of a certain cause."[23]

On at least one occasion, the mistress of a British officer provided the American army with valuable information. Major Patrick Ferguson, the young Scottish commander of loyalist troops, brought his two "cooks" with him to the battle of King's Mountain, South Carolina. One of these young women, known as Virginia Sal, was killed early in the battle. But Ferguson's other mistress, Virginia

90

Paul, abandoned the British forces as the battle turned against them, and helped an American officer identify and target the major. When the battle was over, Virginia Sal was buried with the slain Major Ferguson but Virginia Paul rode out of camp with the other prisoners, appearing, it was said, remarkably unconcerned about her lover's death.[24]

Modern readers are more likely to think of Virginia Paul or the prostitutes of Holy Ground when they hear the term "camp followers." But Sarah Osborn, who cooked meals for Washington's soldiers during the Yorktown bombardment; Sally St. Clair, who died fighting at the siege of Charleston; the nurses who scoured hospital floors with vinegar and tended to sick and wounded men; the washerwomen who earned two shillings for a vest; and the nameless women of Pennsylvania's 6th Regiment who brought water to their soldiers in the heat of battle must redefine the term for us. The Hessian wives and the tag, rag, and bobtail women of the middle states' regiments may have appeared a "sordid set of creatures," but a British army officer saw through the dirt and grime: "if [we] had destroyed all the men in North America," he said, "we should have enough to do to conquer the women."[25]

CHAPTER 5

"HOW UNHAPPY IS WAR TO DOMESTIC HAPPINESS"

Generals' Wives and the War

When a small, dark-haired widow named Martha Dandridge Custis married the tall, handsome Mr. Washington in 1759, she expected to live a comfortable, quiet life as a devoted wife and a doting mother. Her husband expected a similar domestic existence. "I am now I believe fixd at this Seat with an agreeable Consort for life," he wrote an English friend, "and hope to find more happiness in retirement than I ever experienced amid a wide and bustling World." It was not to be. Within a few years, the tensions between Great Britain and the colonies had begun to mount, and by 1775, George Washington was at the center of events in that "wide and bustling World." The world around Martha Washington changed as well. Content to be a matron in rural Virginia, she became a camp follower of the Continental Army.[1]

Of course, neither Martha Washington nor any American general's wife trudged behind the supply wagons or earned a few pennies a day washing the dirty linens of the soldiers. They would never sleep in a tent or in a hastily constructed hut, scavenge for food, or tear boots off a dying soldier. Instead, the generals' wives would spend their time at the winter encampments in the most comfortable housing the army could provide, and there they would serve as hostesses at dinner parties for the officers and attend social events planned by other generals' wives and daughters. Their value to the army was symbolic rather than practical. A general's wife lifted the morale of her husband, his officers, and his troops. She represented the prosperous and genteel life that officers were fighting to defend—and that many soldiers hoped would be theirs if America won its independence. Her presence, even under privileged conditions, was a declaration that everyone, even wealthy wives and mothers, was willing to make sacrifices for the Revolution.

Unlike the "sordid set of creatures" who made up the majority of the camp followers, Martha Washington was not driven to the army by poverty, hunger, or fear. Her only motive was a sense of duty, for as a wife she believed herself bound to accede to her husband's wishes. As she put it in a letter to her brother-in-law, the matter was a simple one: "[if] he will send for me . . . I must go." And it was this obligation, softened by a genuine affection for her husband, that led her to travel hundreds of miles, over snow-covered roads and rain-swollen rivers, to join George Washington each winter of the war.[2]

The news that so dramatically changed Martha Washington's life came in a letter from her husband on June 18, 1775. He was away from home, attending the second Continental Congress in Philadelphia, when he wrote that he had been appointed commander of the "whole Army raised for the defence of the American Cause." George assured Martha that he had not sought the position and that he would "enjoy more happiness and felicity in one month with you, at home, than I have the most distant prospect of reaping abroad, if my stay were to be Seven times seven years." Yet, both husband and wife knew that he could not, would not, refuse. "I cannot blame him," she wrote years later, "for having acted according to his ideas of duty in obeying the voice of his country."[3]

In the beginning, Martha prepared herself for a separation of uncertain length from her husband of fifteen years. In the same letter that he reported his appointment, George had urged her to do whatever she thought might produce a "tolerable degree of Tranquillity" for her while he was away. He urged her to move to Alexandria if she wanted to be nearer her friends, or to pass the time with a round of visits to family and friends across Virginia. Her "fortitude" and "Resolution" would not only sustain her, he added, but it would ease his mind. He did not want to learn that she was "dissatisfied, and complaining at what I really could not avoid." General Washington need not have worried for it was not in his wife's character to complain. "I am . . . determined to be cheerful and happy in whatever situation I may be," she once wrote, and, on the whole, this is how people found her.[4]

Martha Washington might have spent the war, as many wives of political leaders, diplomats, and military men, spent it: at home, waiting. Such was the fate of Deborah Franklin, who died while her husband, Benjamin, was in France. And such was the fate of Abigail Adams, who sent her son off to Europe with her diplomat husband in 1779, but did not risk the Atlantic crossing herself for five more years. As the war stretched into years rather than months, Martha would certainly have missed her husband's companionship as these two wives missed theirs. Yet Martha Washington was, in the modern vernacular, a homebody. She doted on "Jacky" Custis, the only remaining child of her first marriage, and she relished the role of sister and aunt to her extended family in Virginia. Until the war, she had not ventured far from home, either in reality or through the reading of literature, history, or newspapers. Her education had been limited, as befit a planter's daughter. She could read and write—although her spelling was atrocious— and she had learned to cook and sew and to dance. She was, by 1775, a dignified matron, with no evident craving for adventure and no desire to be in the public eye. But soon after he took command of the Continental troops in 1775, General Washington apparently changed his mind about an extended separation and instructed his wife to join him. That November, Martha journeyed to the encampment outside Boston—the first of the many trips she would make to military camps.

As the wife of the commander in chief of the Continental Army, Martha Washington was immediately treated as a celebrity. When she stopped at Philadelphia on the way to Massachusetts, she was warmly greeted and lavishly entertained for a week. The attention both surprised and amused her. Writing to a friend at home that December, she said: "I don't doubt but you have seen the Figuer [figure] our arrival made in the Philadelphia paper—and I left it in as great pomp as if I had been a very great somebody." On December 11, she finally reached Massachusetts, where once again her position as the commander's wife ensured her special treatment. She was settled into a comfortable house in Cambridge that had been confiscated from a loyalist merchant. But no amount of hospitality could make her feel entirely comfortable. Writing home, she confided to her sister that she found the people of Massachusetts strangely "cheerfull and happy" despite the gravity of their situation, and she marveled at how calmly they took the periodic bombardment by cannon coming out of Boston. The cannon fire "does not seem to surprise any one but me; I confess I shudder every time I hear the sound of a gun." All the preparations for war frightened her, but, she added, "I endeavor to keep my fears to myself as well as I can."[5]

She hid her fears well. Those who met Martha that winter did not see a frightened, homesick woman. A soldier who met her wrote in his diary that "Mrs Washington combines in an uncommon degree great dignity of manner with the most pleasing affability," although he conceded that she possessed "no striking marks of beauty." And Abigail Adams, who in later years would be less complimentary, wrote, "Mrs Washington is one of those unassuming characters which create Love and Esteem." An aide to the Prussian drillmaster Baron von Steuben later likened Martha to "the Roman matrons of whom I had read so much," saying, "I thought that she well deserved to be the companion and friend of the greatest man of the age."[6]

For the next eight years, Martha Washington would be a fixture in the Continental Army camps. In 1776, she was in New York, until the impending British attack convinced her husband to send her to the safety of Philadelphia. In early 1778, she was at Valley Forge, where her husband, distressed by their small quarters and aware of the burden of entertaining placed upon Martha, had a log cabin built in which he and his officers could dine. During the frigid months at Valley Forge, Martha made her way through snow and slush to visit with other elite camp followers like General Nathanael Greene's wife, Caty, and the formidable Lucy Knox. The following winter she was at Middlebrook, where she watched, apparently contentedly, as Caty Greene and her own husband danced for three hours at one of the many parties given for the officers. In 1780, she was at Morristown and in 1781 at the American camp in New Jersey. Wherever she went, she impressed those who saw her as an amiable, unpretentious woman, who could usually be found knitting or sewing for her husband and his troops. The officers and their wives, as well as the soldiers, found her behavior impeccable. Her only risqué act, it would seem, was to slyly acknowledge the young Alexander Hamilton's reputation as a ladies' man by naming a stray tomcat after him at Valley Forge.

Martha confided little to the wives and daughters of her husband's fellow officers or to correspondents from the Northeast. She sent friendly notes to Mercy Otis Warren, who had extended hospitality to her that first winter with the army in Boston, congratulating Warren on the evacuation of that city by the British and reporting that the general was well. But Martha Washington sometimes revealed her feelings to her family and friends. Few letters remain, but those that do speak openly of her desire to be at home and in the company of her loved ones. Writing to her sister on August 28, 1776, from the safety of Philadelphia, she explained, "I am still in this town and Noe prospects of my leveing it," adding that she "most religiously wish thare was an End to the matter that we might have the pleasure of meeting again."Although she knew, as all eighteenth-century Americans knew, that mail was unreliable, she sometimes worried she had been forgotten by her family. Writing to her son and daughter-in-law from the encampment at Middlebrook in March 1779, she let her anxiety get the best of her: "If you do not write," she threatened, "I will not write to you again."[7]

A yearning to be home and a concern for the welfare of her husband were the only problems that plagued Martha Washington until the spring of 1781. As she was preparing to leave the New Windsor encampment, she was stricken with abdominal pains and jaundice, symptoms that suggest a gallbladder infection. She was ill for five weeks, and was forced to remain at New Windsor although her husband had already departed with his troops. The illness prompted a strange episode and one of the few instances of inconsiderate behavior on the general's part.

While Martha was sick, the British intercepted several of the letters she wrote to her absent husband. Somehow these letters came into the hands of Martha Mortier, the widow of a paymaster in the British army. Learning that the general's wife was having difficulty procuring "some Necessary Articles for her recovery," Mortier decided to help. She sent, among other things, a box of lemons, a box of oranges, four boxes of sweetmeats, a keg of tamarinds, two dozen pineapples, and two pounds of Hyson tea, all under a special flag of truce from British-occupied New York City. Martha's response to this act of kindness is unknown, but George Washington's was clear: he ordered his men to reject the flag of truce and return the goods to his wife's benefactor. His decision is puzzling, for throughout the war, generals on both sides of the conflict extended hospitality and assistance to enemies of similar rank, and courtesies to the wives of high-ranking officers were equally common. When, for example, the British officer Lord Acland was injured and captured during one of the battles at Saratoga, the Americans permitted Lady Harriet Acland to come into their camp to nurse her husband back to health. Perhaps Washington, a man who was always conscious of his social class, resented that a paymaster's widow had been privy to personal letters between him and his wife.[8]

Without the benefit of oranges or lemons or Hyson tea, Martha Washington at last recovered and returned to Virginia at the end of June. By October, the British army at Yorktown had surrendered to the combined forces of her husband and the French Admiral Rochambeau, and the war she had religiously wished would come to an end was at last over. Ironically, it was peace that brought Martha Washington the only profound personal tragedy of the war. Her adored son, Jacky Custis, had avoided participation in the Revolution until the celebrations by French and American officers after the victory at Yorktown drew him to join the social life of the camp. There he contracted one of the many strains of camp fever and died. The general had made it safely through the war, but Martha's only remaining child had not.

For Martha Washington, the yearly trips to the army camps were a matter of duty, both to the husband she loved and to the cause he espoused. No one who knew Martha's contentment at home in Virginia would have suggested that she found the long winters at Valley Forge or Morristown pleasurable. But Martha was not typical of the American generals' wives. Many were younger and few had the deeply satisfying and extensive roots in their community that Martha enjoyed. Lucy Knox, the wife of twenty-seven-year-old General Henry Knox, had no family left in her hometown of Boston, for both her parents had left with the British as loyalist refugees. Although Lucy made the best of the wartime separation from her "Harry," friends and acquaintances could not fill the void of a husband's absence. "I return home," she wrote Henry, "to find myself entirely alone, to reflect that the only friend I have in the world is such an immense distance from me. . . . My poor heart is ready to burst." Lonely and restless, Lucy craved an escape from a life she described as "barren of adventure and replete with repetition." She found camp life so invigorating that she resented any effort by her husband to limit her visits to the army. Henry's refusal to let her return to New York as the British invasion began prompted her to challenge the genteel model of the obedient wife. In 1777, in the midst of a discussion of a postwar career in business for her husband, she wrote that "you being long accustomed to command—will make you too haughty for mercantile matters," and then pointedly added: "I hope you will not consider yourself as commander in chief of your own house, but be convinced . . . that there is such a thing as equal command." It is impossible to imagine Martha Washington asserting such a claim.[9]

Catharine Greene, the wife of General Nathanael Greene, presented an even greater contrast to Martha Washington. Caty was a newlywed in 1775, when her husband rode off to join the American forces surrounding Boston. Beautiful, flirtatious, self-absorbed, and not yet twenty years old, Caty took little pleasure in the solitude of her home in rural Rhode Island or in the company of her husband's large family. She welcomed the war as an opportunity for adventure, friendships with prominent women, and the attention and companionship of young officers closer to her age than Nathanael, who was more than a decade her senior. For Caty, the dangers of war added a welcome intensity to the dinner parties and dances organized to distract the men from thoughts of the next campaign.

Many wealthy young women shared Caty Greene's romantic notions of war and relished being surrounded by dashing men in uniform. Sally Wister, tall, blond, and only sixteen, was certainly one of them. Sally's father, a wealthy Quaker merchant, had taken his family out of Philadelphia in 1777 and settled them in a farmhouse fifteen miles from the city. Boring days gave way to excitement for Sally when officers from Maryland, Virginia, and New Jersey regiments appeared at their door. Over the next few months she was able to fill a diary-length letter to a friend with tales of her encounters with young majors and colonels and captains, all of them elegant in red and buff and blue uniforms and wearing swords and sashes. As the British overran Philadelphia, Sally was preoccupied with freshening her "dress and lips" before greeting her guests, and choosing which gown to wear for dinner. She took a particular liking to a nineteen-year-old Maryland major whom she described as "the glory, the Major, so bashful, so famous, &c." but she developed what modern readers would call crushes on older officers as well. For Wister, nothing in life would ever prove as thrilling as these nine months of the Revolution.[10]

Caty Greene might have said the same. Born in 1756, Catharine Littlefield had married Nathanael Greene in 1774, when she was eighteen and he was thirty. They were an odd couple: she with her "high color . . . vivacious expression, and snapping pair of dark eyes"; he somber and dutiful, with "a face indicating fire and firmness, tempered by the innate goodness which looks out of his clear, quiet eyes." Yet it was apparent that Greene adored the woman he called his "dear angel."[11]

Before her husband abandoned his Quaker tenet of pacifism and joined the army, Caty Greene had never shown much interest in the political crisis in the colonies. While redcoats and militia clashed at Lexington and Concord, Caty's thoughts were on her first pregnancy. It was not until Nathanael rode off to Massachusetts that she began to follow developments in local Rhode Island newspapers. Despite her pregnancy, she longed to see the events unfolding for herself, so much so that in the spring she climbed into her carriage and made the full day's ride to the American army camp. She was shocked and disappointed by what she saw, for the Rhode Island troops were not smartly dressed, disciplined soldiers but a disorganized and disrespectful group of farm boys who ignored her husband's commands, laughed at orders, and sulked if too much was demanded of them.

Nathanael Greene, by now elevated to the rank of brigadier general, did not think an army camp a proper place for his young wife. In viewing her as a delicate, sensitive female, to be protected from the harsher realities of life, Nathanael embodied the genteel eighteenth-century notions of gender. Thus by June Caty had been sent back to their Coventry home, where she was once again lonely and miserable. When a friend of theirs was killed by cannon fire, Nathanael seemed more firmly convinced than ever that he was correct to shelter her from the violent scenes of war. Indeed, Nathanael feared the impact that news of this tragedy would have on his wife's delicate sensibility. "My dear angel," he wrote, "the anxiety that you must feel at the unhappy fate of Mr. Mumford, the tender sympathy for the distress of his poor lady . . . the fears and apprehensions for my safety, under your present debilitated state, must be a weight too great for you to support. . . . Stiffle your grief, my sweet creature."[12]

But Caty was made of sterner stuff than her husband suspected and she pressed him every winter for permission to escape from the tedium of life with his brother and sister-in-law or visits to his parents. Each time Nathanael gave in to her pleas, she rushed with delight to Providence to purchase new clothes for her trip. This ritual shopping spree made her, no doubt, the best-dressed general's wife in the American camp.

If Martha Washington regarded the approach of winter with a touch of dread, Caty Greene clearly looked forward to it with anticipation. Throughout their marriage, Nathanael considered his wife fragile and in need of comforting, yet Caty was sometimes recklessly brave and always resourceful. In her various yearly efforts to join her husband, little seemed to deter her. On the verge of childbirth, she trusted her fate to the army doctors near

Boston. Frightened of sailing, and in danger of capture by a British patrol boat, she nevertheless took a boat across the Long Island Sound to get to New York City before the British attack. Facing a long journey along rutted roads and several nights in shabby inns along the way, she climbed in her carriage with her son and traveled from Coventry to Philadelphia to meet her husband. Her rewards were an intense social life and, in February 1778, the pleasure of dancing the night away with none other than the commander in chief.

The truth was that army life was a perfect antidote to Caty's boredom. At Valley Forge and in New York City, in Basking Ridge and Middlebrook, New Jersey, she found herself at the center of a social circle that included the Washingtons, General Horatio Gates and his wife Elizabeth, Thomas and Sarah Mifflin, and later, Lucy and Henry Knox and the self-titled Lord Stirling's family. As many of the army officers in the camps were bachelors, Caty also had the pleasure of innocent flirting with men her own age.

Nathanael did everything he could to assure his dear angel the best circumstances wherever the army's winter quarters might be. Perhaps his greatest success in accommodating his wife came when the Continental troops encamped at Morristown, New Jersey. General Greene arranged an invitation for Caty to stay at the home of William Alexander, Lord Stirling. The Stirling estate at

Basking Ridge was a showplace, with lawns, gardens, vineyards, stables, and a deer-filled park, and Lady Stirling and her daughters were eager to play hostess to Caty. When Nathanael and his soldiers were forced to retreat in the face of General Howe's army, taking flight from Philadelphia and driven back at Brandywine, Caty chose to settle in at Basking Ridge. A twelve-month separation from Nathanael followed, during which he poured out his longing for his wife. "Oh my sweet angel," he wrote, "how I wish—how I long to return to your soft embrace. The endearing prospect is my greatest comfort amidst all the fatigues of the campaign." Caty missed her husband as well, but she filled her evenings with dancing parties, partnering with the unmarried officers who remained stationed nearby.[13]

The following year at Valley Forge, Caty found that social opportunities compensated for the dismal conditions in camp. She made daily rounds, visiting Martha Washington, Lucy Knox, and the Stirling women. Nathanael had managed to find her comfortable quarters three miles away from the main camp, and here she opened her home to a steady stream of officers, including the eccentric Anthony Wayne and Nathanael's young and handsome fellow officer, Jeremiah Wadsworth. Gossip at last began to spread about Caty Greene, but her doting husband ignored it—and probably rightly so. Caty enjoyed the company of men, but there is no evidence that she was unfaithful to Nathanael.[14]

The separation from his wife during the active campaign months continued to sadden Nathanael Greene. "How unhappy is war to domestic happiness," he wrote in the summer of 1780. Now that the war had carried him south, where a second major British campaign had begun, he urged Caty to make the best of the situation. He wrote to her again, suggesting two alternatives during his absence: she could retire to their farm at Westerly or remain at Coventry. After years of instructing her as if she were a child, yet often caving in to her pleas, Nathanael was making the effort to share the decision about her immediate future with his wife. Yet he continued to assume that her choices were limited to what he himself would approve. "In a word," he concluded, "choose for yourself and act for yourself. . . . I have full confidence you will do nothing but [what] will be perfectly to my liking." But given an inch, Caty took a mile. She chose neither of his suggestions. Instead, true to her own temperament, she spent her days in Newport, Rhode Island, enjoying the company of the French officers stationed there under Rochambeau.[15]

Nathanael Greene went on to remarkable success and fame during the second southern campaign of the war. But he did not see his wife again until after the British surrender at Yorktown. In December 1781, Caty Greene journeyed south, stopping in Philadelphia to visit with General Washington. Despite the tragedy that had just occurred in his own family life—the death of Martha's son—Washington made a special effort to see that Caty was treated well. He would, he assured Nathanael, "endeavor to strew the way with flowers" for his general's wife.[16]

At last, in April 1782, Caty reached South Carolina and the Greenes were reunited. Caty, now the mother of four, was still youthful, but at thirty-eight Nathanael seemed a tired old man. Seeing her husband's face, lined with wrinkles, Caty realized how brutal the Revolution had been in the South. Here, Americans had fought Americans, in a war that was as much a civil war as a struggle for independence. But the worst days of the war were over, and in October, General Greene and his troops made a triumphant march into the reclaimed city of Charleston. With them, resplendent in a dress the color of a Continental uniform, trimmed with yellow buttons and buff-colored facing, was Caty Greene. Afterward, her husband wrote with genuine pride that his wife was "much esteemed by both the Army and the people, as well as loved and admired by her husband." Nathanael too was much esteemed. The state of South Carolina granted him rich farmlands—a gesture of thanks for the liberation of the state from British and loyalist hands. Four years later, however, Nathanael was dead, and Caty Greene had embarked on a new life as a plantation mistress.[17]

Martha Washington and Caty Greene had few counterparts in the British army. British generals preferred camp wives to real wives, often taking as their mistresses the wives of junior officers. Sir William Howe had his "Sultana," Mrs. Loring; General John Burgoyne had his paymaster's wife. But the Hessian general, Friedrich Adolf Riedesel, did not follow the same customs as his British employers. His wife came to America in 1777 and left behind a journal of her long and often harrowing odyssey from a small German town to the battlefields of the Hudson Valley and a detailed record of her life as a prisoner of war after the British defeat at Saratoga.

Frederika Charlotte Louise von Massow, the Baroness von Riedesel, was young and attractive like Caty Greene. Like Caty, she had once paraded down the streets of an American city. But the baroness had not been marching in triumph. She was, instead, a prisoner of war. While Hannah Winthrop did not see the redheaded Frederika among the "beasts of burden" following Burgoyne's defeated army, the baroness was indeed among the almost two thousand women who had been present when the British surrendered at Saratoga. Frederika's experience was unique and filled with sharp contrasts: she was a privileged general's wife who saw the horrors of the battlefield firsthand and spent almost four years as a prisoner of war.[18]

Frederika was only sixteen in 1762 when she married a handsome twenty-four-year-old cavalry officer, Fritz Riedesel, the Baron of Eisenbach, and moved with him to the town of Wolfenbuttel. In

110

her early years as the baron's wife, she looked more like "an unmarried girl who is just being brought to boarding school," a friend observed, "instead of . . . a married woman." But Frederika was already a veteran of war and the demanding life of the army camp. Her father had been a career soldier, a lieutenant general in the Prussian army, and, as a child, Frederika had frequently traveled with him and his troops. More than any of the American generals' wives, the Baroness von Riedesel knew the rigors of being a camp follower.[19]

It is doubtful that the Riedesels followed the tensions developing between Great Britain and its colonies, but, in their fourteenth year of marriage, their fates became intertwined with the future of Britain's empire. That year, 1776, King George III signed agreements with the princes of three German provinces—Brunswick, Hesse-Kassel, and Hesse-Hanau—who agreed to send regiments to support the British suppression of the American rebellion. As a professional soldier, the baron viewed this arrangement as a career opportunity. And so it was. He was named commander of the first contingent from Brunswick to sail for America and was immediately elevated from the rank of colonel to major general. Pleased with his promotion, he began to address his wife as "Mrs. General."[20]

"Mrs. General" was eight months pregnant when her husband set out in February 1776 on the long land and ocean journey to the Hessian

111

staging ground in Canada. But it was understood that, as soon as she and the baby could travel, she too would leave Wolfenbuttel for America. Even with the promise of a reunion before the year was out, both Riedesels were miserable at the separation. "Never have I known greater suffering than upon my departure this morning," wrote Fritz, and Frederika expressed her relief that her husband had given her permission to follow him.[21]

The general continued to write to his wife as he traveled across Belgium and into England. Assuming the prerogative of a husband to tell his wife when to travel and how, what to bring and whom to contact along the way, Fritz filled his letters with instructions he expected Frederika to dutifully obey. From on board ship and from Canada, he tried to manage her every move. "Dearest Angel," he wrote on March 26, 1776, "remember that everyone gets sick at sea and that your servants cannot do a thing for you. You must, therefore, take the shortest crossing, and I consider the best way is from Calais. . . ." He insisted that she could not make the transatlantic crossing without the companionship of another respectable matron, the wife of an English captain named Foy. "You must wait patiently for the directions Captain Foy will give you and you will have nothing to risk . . . rest calm and content."[22]

Although Frederika was obedient, she was far from incompetent or childlike. Like her husband, she kept her purse strings tightly drawn, budgeting money carefully and, whenever possible, seizing opportunities to improve their fortunes. Writing to her mother in May, just before her departure from Wolfenbuttel, she explained that she was bringing a number of antiques with her to England since the market there for German items was excellent. In other letters to her mother, she gave practical advice on the sale of land and the advantages of marrying her younger sister to a wealthy man.[23]

The Riedesels' third daughter was born in March 1776, while Fritz was at sea. By May, the baroness, with Gustava, four years old, Frederica, two, and the ten-week-old Carolina, was on her way to England. Frederika admitted in her journal that "I still felt the greatness of my undertaking too much not to have a heavy heart." She had been told frightening stories of cannibalism among the Canadian Indians and been assured that people in America subsisted on a diet of "horse-flesh and cats," but it was not these images that distressed her. It was "the thought of going into a country where I could not understand the language" that caused her anxiety. The baroness kept her anxiety to herself, for she was traveling with three small children who depended on her for their safety and their sense of security. Along the way she faced challenges enough. Early in the trip, they passed through a forest rumored to be filled with robbers. As twilight came, the body of one of their victims, hanging from one of the branches overhead, struck the baroness through the open window of the carriage. That evening, they took shelter in a building she suspected was a robbers' den. Unable to go farther until daylight returned, she left her servant, Rockel, to stand guard outside their door, and gathered up her daughters to sleep beside her. Later, as they prepared to board the boat at Calais for the Channel crossing, her girls became frightened. Recalling this later on in her journal, she said simply: "I pretended to be very courageous in order to dispel their fears."[24]

Frederika and her family arrived in London on June 1, 1776, but they did not remain long. The baron had instructed his wife to go as soon as possible from London to Bristol, where she was to connect with Captain Foy's wife. But both Bristol and Mrs. Foy proved disastrous. Neither the baroness nor her servants could speak a word of English, nor did they understand the customs of an English seaport town. The baroness was insulted on the street by sailors who assumed from her clothing that she was a prostitute, and she was ridiculed by several respectable townspeople for putting ribbons in her daughters' hair. At first, all she could do was hide in her room and weep. Yet after a few days she dried her tears and began an intensive study of English. Within six weeks, she knew enough of the language—and the local dress code—to cope with Bristol.[25]

Nothing could help her cope with Mrs. Foy, however. The captain's wife had not yet received written permission from her husband to travel—and so she would not budge, despite the need to make the transatlantic crossing before cold weather set in. Even when the letter came, Mrs. Foy hesitated, clearly preferring to remain at home rather than go to Canada. Frederika's husband had flooded her with instructions on everything from whom to contact in London, to how to choose a ship for the voyage, to what foods and supplies to bring on board, but he had not told her how to deal with a woman whose indecision sabotaged every effort to depart. Frustrated, but helpless because of her husband's determination that she travel with the captain's wife, Frederika was forced to spend almost a year in England.

At last, on April 15, 1777, the Riedesel family boarded a ship at Portsmouth for an eight-week voyage to Canada. There were days of seasickness, but there were also days so sunny and calm that the baroness and her children "danced upon deck" to the music of a fifer and three drummers. Their ship was part of a large convoy that was protected by British naval vessels that carried several regiments of German troops as well. These soldiers gave the baroness an indication of the high esteem in which they held her husband, for, as a ship carrying over a hundred Hessians passed close by, the men raised their flag and called out, "Long live the dear wife of our general, and the good general himself!" In gratitude, Frederika lifted her children so that they could wave to the men.[26]

During the voyage, the baroness confided little in her journal about the war itself. She had apparently expressed some sympathy for the Americans in a letter to her husband, for he reprimanded her in June 1776. The Revolution, he wrote, echoing the loyalist argument, was the work of a dozen ambitious men whose lust for power made "the whole land unhappy." He had nothing but contempt for both the ringleaders and their dupes, who he said did not even know why they were fighting. Having seen some captured rebels only a few weeks earlier, he assured his wife that they were little more than "poor rascals" who could do him no harm. In fact, by September 1776, he was convinced that the entire war would be over within a year. The English and Hessian forces would invade New England from Canada when spring came, and "by then, the whole affair will be finished." Believing that his wife was already sailing to Canada when he wrote this in the summer of 1776, Fritz thought they would be sailing home again, together, by 1778.[27]

Fritz's predictions would soon prove terribly wrong. But in June 1777, the Riedesels were too delighted by the brief reunion they at last enjoyed to concern themselves with military outcomes. The general, who was called away soon after Frederika arrived, had found accommodations for his wife and daughters at Trois-Rivières, or Three Rivers, a little village much less expensive than Montreal or Quebec. In August, he sent word that his family could join him on the ambitious New

York campaign. Soon the baroness and her children, riding in a small open carriage called a calash, were following General Burgoyne's army on its slow march through Canada and New York. Although the campaign began well, this effort to control the Hudson Valley and thus separate New England from the rest of the rebellious colonies proved disastrous. By early September, supplies were running dangerously low, and most of the army's Indian allies had abandoned them. This left Burgoyne with few scouts and little information on the movements of his enemy. On the other hand, the baroness was certain that the Americans were receiving full reports on Burgoyne's army. In her journal, she noted with shock how lax the British commander was about security. Civilians, she wrote, wandered freely about the camp, pretending to be loyalists, but she believed they reported on the size and condition of the invading force to the Americans.[28]

On September 19, 1777, the first of the Saratoga battles was fought near a clearing called Freeman's Farm. The baroness was there. "I was an eye witness of the whole affair," she wrote, and "I could hear everything." Knowing that her husband was in the thick of battle, she was unable to maintain her usual calm. "I was full of care and anguish, and shivered at every shot." Soon the wounded came pouring into the farmhouse where she and her girls and the wives of several other officers had taken cover. Among the wounded was an English officer, not yet twenty years old, from a family who had been kind to Frederika during her stay in London. The baroness did what she could to comfort him, providing him with food and pillows, blankets, and a mattress. Despite her efforts, the young man died. She could hear his death groans, she recalled, through the thin partition between her room and his.[29]

Burgoyne's troops and the German soldiers under Riedesel managed to hold their ground and thus claim victory. But rather than pursue the American forces under the lethargic General Horatio Gates, the equally lackadaisical British commander decided to allow his men a day's rest. Burgoyne then delayed further, operating on the misguided notion that General Clinton was on his way with reinforcements from New York City. With only about five thousand battle-ready troops, most of them hungry and all of them weary, officers like the baron grew pessimistic. The baroness was painfully aware of the condition of the troops, for many of the officers had come begging a meal from her since the battle at Freeman's Farm.

On the evening of October 7, the baroness was preparing for dinner when she heard sounds of a skirmish nearby. Soon soldiers rushed in, carrying General Simon Fraser, who had been mortally wounded. Immediately, the dinner table was removed and a bed set up for the Englishman in the center of the room. Once again, Frederika's thoughts turned to her own husband. "I sat in a corner of the room trembling and quaking," she wrote, "The thought that they might bring in my husband in the same manner was to me dreadful, and tormented me incessantly." Fritz remained unharmed, but the baroness's house filled with other sick and wounded soldiers. That evening her husband quietly warned her to prepare to flee. She was to keep her preparations secret, giving no one "the least inkling of what I was doing." The following morning, she awoke to find the dead General Fraser, wrapped in a sheet, lying on the bedstead in the dining room for all to see.[30]

That day, Burgoyne suddenly decided to decamp and move his army northward. Frederika was forced to move quickly in order to follow the departing troops. Fearing that the slightest sound would alert the enemy to her flight, she stuffed a cloth in the mouth of one of her daughters to stifle the girl's crying. The campaign, begun so gloriously, now seemed doomed. The blame, both Fritz and Frederika agreed, lay firmly on the shoulders of the British commander, who valued his pleasures more than he did his responsibilities. At crucial moments Burgoyne had lingered to enjoy eating and drinking—and sex with his mistress—when he should have been moving his army to a better strategic position. Other German soldiers shared their view. As one reported: "While the army were suffering from cold and hunger, and every one was looking forward to the immediate future with apprehension . . . there Burgoyne was sitting, with some merry companions, at a dainty supper, while the champagne was flowing."[31]

The baroness was so enraged by Burgoyne's behavior that she breached the standards of feminine behavior: shortly before the final battle at Saratoga, she sent an officer to remind the commander that his men were starving. When Burgoyne, clearly annoyed by the implied criticism, thanked her profusely for reminding him of his duty, Frederika refused to excuse his negligence. "I begged his pardon for having meddled with things which, I well knew, a woman had no business with," she wrote, but said "it was impossible to keep silent, when I saw so many brave men in want of every thing. . . ." But a decent meal would no longer raise the spirits of the young officers whom she had sustained with tea and coffee and what little food she could spare. During the night, several of these men came to her, giving her their money, watches, and rings for safekeeping against their death in the battle ahead.[32]

In the next few days, the baroness saw more death and suffering, and her own children almost became casualties of the war. The baron sent her to a house not far from the army's new encampment, but American soldiers fired on her carriage as she and her daughters made their way to its shelter. Soon after they arrived, a cannonade struck the house. The Americans may have believed that this was the British commander's headquarters, but in truth there was no one inside except the sick, the wounded, and women and children. As the attack continued, Frederika took charge. She moved everyone to the cellar where "a horrible stench, the cries of the children, and yet more than all this, my own anguish" kept her awake through the night. In the morning, she ordered everyone upstairs, despite the continuing danger, so that she could clean the cellar, for it had been "soiled" by women and children too frightened to relieve themselves aboveground.[33]

After scouring what she could, she called everyone back downstairs. The cellar, she discovered, was actually composed of three separate rooms, and so she began to reorganize its occupants. The most dangerously wounded she put in one, women in another, and the rest in the third. A German soldier recalled the scene in "these dens of wretchedness": "There," he wrote, "was . . . Lady Riedesel with her tender infants . . . amidst the suffering and despairing. The dismal space was thronged, and the air . . . quite infected.—the extraordinary German woman preserved her courage and compassion. She acted then the part of an angel of comfort and help among the sufferers. She refreshed them with what she had left of provisions. . . . By her energy she restored order in that chaos. . . ."[34]

When everyone was at last settled, Frederika's thoughts turned to her husband, who she knew was now engaged in battle. "I was more dead than alive," she wrote, "though not so much on account of our own danger, as for that which enveloped my husband." When the truce came between the two armies, she realized that she was the only woman in the cellars whose husband was neither dead nor wounded.[35]

On October 17, 1777, the capitulation of the British army was completed. Gates and Burgoyne agreed to a "convention" rather than a "surrender" and thus technically the defeated army were not prisoners of war. The plan was that the troops and their dependents would march to Boston and from there be transported home. In return, they pledged not to take up arms in the American conflict again. Soon afterward, however, the American Congress and General Washington rejected the terms. Washington, afraid that the returning soldiers would be used to free up new troops for service in America, insisted that the Hessian and the English prisoners remain on American soil. The decision had serious consequences: the British refused to pay for the supplies and shelter of the captured men, leaving them to the mercy of a penniless American government.

These problems lay in the future, however. In late October, the baroness's greatest fear was the treatment she and her children would receive at the hands of their captors. She was relieved to discover that the American officers knew how to behave to a lady. When she arrived in the American camp with her husband, General Philip Schuyler greeted her, saying, "Fear nothing," and led her to the tent where General Horatio Gates himself was waiting. Here, she found the commanding officers of the two opposing armies amiably conversing. Burgoyne rose, saying to her: "You may now dismiss all your apprehensions, for your sufferings are at an end." So, apparently, were his, for that evening the American, British, and Hessian generals all dined together.[36]

General Schuyler opened his own house in Albany to the baroness and her children, and there they stayed until the defeated British and Hessian troops and their camp followers began the long march to Boston. Frederika recorded that the disasters of the campaign had not destroyed her "frolicksomeness" or her spirits, but she saw the toll defeat had taken upon her husband. He was "gnawed by grief on account of all that had happened," and he had become "peevish in the highest degree."[37]

Although the American officers had behaved honorably, Frederika did meet with some hostility when she first arrived in Boston. Her first land-lady showed her contempt for the Hessian family by combing lice out of her own daughter's hair at the dining table. All five of the Riedesels were crammed into one room of the house, with their maids and manservants forced to sleep on the floor outside the bedroom door. But the situation was temporary. By spring, they were settled into a spacious and elegant home in Cambridge, and in early June Frederika was able to give a ball and an elaborate supper in honor of her husband's birthday. In defeat, her social life now closely resembled that of Martha Washington and Caty Greene.[38]

By the winter of 1778, the burden of providing food and housing for Burgoyne's troops had become too much for the Bostonians. The Hessian prisoners were ordered to the Virginia countryside, where, it was assumed, food would be more abundant and huts and cabins could be constructed to house them. Frederika took the news calmly, but she worried about the effect of the move on Fritz, who was still deeply depressed by "the grief of being in captivity, the unpleasant situation of our troops, and the want of news from his fatherland." The trip south did little to raise his spirits. All along the way, they encountered bad roads, covered with frost, and a cold wind that whipped around their wagon. The people they encountered were equally unpleasant. The Riedesel family was refused food by a woman who considered the Hessians no better than hired killers. "You shall not have a morsel," she told the Riedesels. "Now you are our prisoners; it is, therefore, our turn to torment you." Other women expressed the hope that the family would die of hunger—a wish that often seemed close to fulfillment.[39]

At last, in February 1779, after twelve weeks and 678 miles, the general, his family, and his troops reached their destination in Virginia. The Riedesels paid to have a large house built for them, with an ample drawing room and two side rooms. Although their surroundings were comfortable, the expense of life as a gentleman prisoner of war and the Virginia heat deepened Fritz's depression. His only respite was to work in his garden. One day, under the hot summer sun, he collapsed, probably from a heart attack. He was carried into the house, his face blue, his hands white, his eyes fixed, and his body bathed in sweat. For the remainder of their time in America, Frederika acted as a full-time nurse to her husband. Until he was safely returned to his homeland, the baron could not sleep unless she remained awake beside him.

In August 1779, Fritz received word that he and an English officer were, at last, to be exchanged for two American prisoners. The family headed toward New York City, only to learn that the exchange had been rescinded. The baron was heartbroken, but his English counterpart, General William Phillips, was furious. When Phillips asked Frederika why she did not complain, her reply revealed her character: "Everyone . . . shows his sorrow in his own fashion. . . . I keep mine in my heart." By this time, she had much reason for sorrow: her husband was ill, depressed, and demanding of her time; her daughter Caroline had fallen sick; and she was pregnant again.[40]

It was not until November 1779 that the Riedesels were finally allowed to go to New York City. Here, they were entertained by Governor

William Tryon and General Henry Clinton, and invited to spend the winter months at Clinton's country estate. When she returned to New York, Frederika and her family moved into a house elegantly furnished by the governor. Although she was far along in her fourth pregnancy, Frederika agreed to serve as queen of a ball given to honor the queen of England's birthday. Soon after the ball, Frederika's fourth daughter was born. Thomas Jefferson, who had befriended the Riedesels during their stay in Virginia, sent Fritz his condolences on the birth of yet another female child. But the Riedesels expressed their gratitude to their friends on both sides of the war by naming their infant America.[41]

Frederika and Fritz established themselves as central figures in the social life of the officer corps. Every week, the Riedesels hosted a gentlemen's dinner party whose guest list included General Phillips and Governor Tryon. But that fall, a smallpox epidemic interrupted their pleasant existence. Fifty people died each day and the Riedesel household did not escape unscathed. Fritz and Gustava fell ill, along with most of the servants. Frederika was left to nurse them all. Her husband was so sick that he asked to be left to die. The doctor and Frederika, who "had neither opportunity nor desire to lie down" throughout the crisis, saved him. Looking back, the baroness wrote modestly of herself: "It is perfectly amazing what mankind can endure, and what I also went through. But I was well, and blessed with a cheerful happy temperament. . . ."[42]

The Riedesels' long American ordeal was coming to an end. In July 1781 they left New York for Canada, where their fifth daughter, named Canada, was born—and died. At long last, in 1783, the family boarded a ship bound for England. Frederika and Fritz were going home.

Shortly before the family left for Canada the baron had taken his wife with him to review the English troops still officially under his command. When they arrived in the camp, the men greeted Frederika von Riedesel with military honors. Startled, she observed that "we German women were not accustomed to such distinctions." But an English officer replied that his men would never forget what she had done for their sick and wounded comrades at Saratoga. In their minds, the general's wife was as much a war hero as her husband.[43]

The praise and affection for Frederika von Riedesel echoed the praise and affection that Caty Greene received from her husband's troops and that Martha Washington received from the men at Valley Forge and Morristown. That they were admired while the ordinary camp followers were often scorned points to the reality of a social hierarchy in eighteenth-century American society as well as in English society. But more was at play here than the simple distinction of the genteel from the lower classes. The camp followers who washed their dirty clothing and scavenged boots for them from the battlefield were part of the military life these men hoped would soon come to an end. But the generals' wives served to distinguish masculine roles from feminine, and by showing courtesy to them the officers and the soldiers reaffirmed that they could still remember, and function in, a world far removed from the brutality and violence of warfare.

CHAPTER 6

"A JOURNEY A CROSSE YE WILDERNESS"

Loyalist Women in Exile

On September 1, 1774, Esther Quincy Sewall looked through her window in horror at the mob gathering outside her Cambridge home. She did not have to ask why these fifty men and boys were there: she knew they wanted her husband, Jonathan. Jonathan was the Massachusetts attorney general and a judge of the Vice Admiralty Courts, a man who had earned a reputation as the king's staunch defender both in the courts and in the local press. The crowd outside his home meant to make an example of him. But the attorney general was in Boston, Esther explained, and she was alone with her two young sons. Go away, she pleaded. No one moved.

Looking out at so many threatening faces, Esther surely recognized some of them as neighbors, friends, or acquaintances. She had been born and raised in Massachusetts, the daughter of one of the oldest and most notable families of the province, and she had married into another family known throughout New England for its judges, scholars, and lawyers. Until 1774, Esther and Jonathan Sewall had no reason to assume that politics would create an irreparable division among the members of their elite social circle. The ties of class, profession, and family seemed too strong to be broken. Esther's sister had, after all, married John Hancock, making Boston's most popular smuggler and the attorney who prosecuted him brothers-in-law, and Jonathan Sewall's closest friend was fellow lawyer John Adams. But by that fall day in 1774, Esther had learned the lesson that other loyalist women would learn: a crisis of political loyalties had rent the fabric of their social world. Even more disturbing was a second revelation: Esther's loyalty to her husband, once a private commitment, had become a political act. Esther Quincy had become a loyalist because she had become Mrs. Jonathan Sewall.

As rocks began to shatter the windows of her home, a desperate but resourceful Esther Sewall offered the mob free access to her husband's wine cellar. After drinking their fill, the men and boys dispersed. But the experience served as a clear warning to the Sewalls that the time had come to choose. John Adams had been correct when he said the die was cast. A year later, the Sewall family was in England, exiles from their native land.[1]

Over the next decade, other prominent loyalist women would realize, as Esther Sewall had realized, that family prestige and personal ties to leaders of the Revolutionary movement would not necessarily protect them. In Philadelphia, Grace Growden Galloway was to learn this lesson in the hardest of ways. Grace's husband, Joseph, had been speaker of the assembly and a leading member of the Continental Congress. But when independence was declared, he would not renounce his allegiance to the king. When the British occupied Philadelphia in 1776, Joseph Galloway played a major role in assisting them. Then when the British evacuated the city and American forces prepared to occupy it, he fled to the safety of New York City. Like other wealthy loyalists, Joseph left his wife behind, hoping that her presence would deter the new state government from confiscating his property. More than most, the Galloways had reason to be confident, for Grace Growden Galloway was the daughter of one of the wealthiest men in Pennsylvania and much of the Galloway property had come into the marriage through Grace herself.

Haughty and proud, Grace Galloway did not expect a mere revolution to alter her status in her community. Neither her husband's politics nor his defection seemed a serious threat to her, for she had been a Growden long before she became a Galloway. But local authorities disagreed. The Pennsylvania government confiscated the Galloway estate, including all the property Grace had inherited from her father. In the journal she kept during the revolutionary years, Grace recorded her confusion and bitterness at the intrusion of a political conflict into her private life. A decade earlier, she had written a cautionary poem, warning women "never get Tyed to a Man / for when once you are yoked / Tis all a Mere Joke / of seeing your freedom again." As former friends turned their backs on her, as men of her social circle helped reduce her to poverty, Grace Galloway discovered how tied her fate was not only to her husband's whims, but to his politics.

Grace did not surrender quietly. Throughout 1778, her journal entries show her determined attempts to separate and recover her dowry property from the rest of her husband's property. She consulted with the few influential men who did not desert her, hoping that they could find the legal loopholes that would preserve her considerable wealth for her only daughter, Betsy. They could not. "Sent for Mr. Dickinson last Night," she recorded on July 22, 1778, "& he tole Me he would look over ye law to see if I cou'd recover My own estate & this evening he came & he told Me I cou'd Not recover dower & he fear'd my income in My estate was forfeited likewise & ye [that] no tryal wou'd be of service." As the reality of her situation pressed upon her, Grace noted with a mixture of fear and resentment: "So I find I am a beggar. . . ."

By August 1778, local authorities were ready to evict Grace from her elegant town house in Philadelphia. She had been expecting "every hour to be turn'd out of doors," a turn of events that was

132

as frightening as it was humiliating. "Where to go I know not. No one will take me in," she wrote. She appealed to local officials to prevent the eviction, but by August 10 they had come to take possession of the house, arriving with a "spanish Merchant & his attendants" who hoped to be its next residents. As the men entered, Grace collapsed. "I was taken very ill & obliged to Lay down & sent them word I cou'd not see them." Yet she heard them moving about her home, invading her privacy. The Spanish merchant added insult to injury by offering Grace the chance to remain in the house after he occupied it, and gallantly—from his perspective—inviting her to "chuse My own bed chamber." After the men departed, she found they had locked her out of her own parlor.

For almost two weeks, Grace continued to resist her eviction. But on August 20, she heard violent knocking at her door. When she refused to open the front door to them, the men went around to the kitchen door and forced it open. Grace, her maids, and her few supporters stood defiantly in the dark entryway, waiting. Among those who entered were a pewterer and a hatter—men who in former days would have shown deference to a woman of her social standing. Now, however, they came as representatives of a new government, with the authority to send her into the streets. Grace challenged them, telling them, "Nothing but force shou'd get me out of My house." But they replied that "they knew how to Manage that & that they wou'd throw my cloaths in ye street." As the confrontation continued, Grace realized that a deep hatred of her husband fortified the resolve of her opponents. They were prepared not only to evict her, but also to drive her from her home without any of her possessions. "They wou'd let Me Have Nothing," she wrote—and she knew it was true. In a final moment of defiance, she again declared that it was her home and only force would drive her out of it. The reply from one of the men was chilling: "He said it was not ye first time he had taken a Lady by the Hand" and dragged her from her house. "Come Mrs Galloway," he added, more courteously, "give me your hand." When she refused, he took hold of her arm and propelled her to the door. Grace demanded to be released, and made her own way to the carriage waiting outside for her.

Grace Galloway lived out the remainder of her days in rented rooms and increasing isolation in America. But her sense of entitlement never abandoned her. On April 20, 1779, she wrote that she had "got My spirit at command" and could laugh at her enemies. She was, she declared, "ye happiest woman in town for I had been stripped & Turn'd out of Doors yet I was still ye same & must be Joseph Galloways Wife & Lawrence Growdons daughter & that it was Not in their power to humble me for I should be Grace Galloway to the last & . . . I had now suffer'd all that they can inflict Upon Me. . . ."[2]

Like Grace Galloway, the wives of wealthy loyalists were often the targets of Revolutionary governments eager to confiscate the property of men they considered traitors. In these seizures of land, homes, furniture, livestock, and other possessions, greed surely played a part in the decision making. But the rich were not the only targets of attack after independence was declared. In 1776, Americans had, as John Adams was also so fond of saying, crossed the Rubicon, and a choice of loyalties pressed upon everyone. Ordinary farmers and city dwellers who actively opposed independence found themselves in a distinct minority. They could not look to local government to protect them, for the patriots had quickly taken charge in most regions, transforming colonial assemblies into independent state legislatures. Local enforcement agencies, known as Committees of Safety, had sprung up across the country to secure—and ensure—commitments to the Revolutionary cause. Men who refused to sign oaths of loyalty to the cause of independence could be arrested or confined to their homes, and their property, too, could be confiscated. Those loyal to the Crown were forced to seek refuge with the British army or to flee to areas outside the control of the revolutionaries. Men and women, rich or poor, who supported the Crown had become outlaws in their own community.

The farmwives who fell victim to vigilante

groups or mobs were rarely targeted because of their own independent acts of treason against the Revolution. Instead, like Esther Sewall and Grace Galloway, these wives or mothers were simply guilty by association. The neighbors who destroyed their homes and seized their possessions viewed them as surrogates for the offending head of household, who in many cases had left home to enlist with the British army. When a mob drove a woman from her farm, destroyed her home, or confiscated her clothing, the participants believed they were striking a blow against an absent enemy: her husband.

Accounts of such attacks can be found in the petitions to the Crown for compensation filed after the war by women like Isabella MacDonald of North Carolina, Sarah Winslow of Massachusetts, and Susannah Marshall of Maryland, all of whom were persecuted because of their husbands' political choices. Diaries and letters and journals also tell of the violence done to women because of the loyalism of their husbands and fathers. Soon after Hannah Ingraham's father, Benjamin, joined the British army, for example, the family's "comfortable farm" was ransacked, and the "rebels" took away all the livestock except one heifer and four sheep. Despite the pleas of Hannah's four-year-old brother, these patriots refused to leave his pet lamb behind. Elizabeth Cary Wilstee faced a similar fate: left to manage the family farm in the New Hampshire grants, Elizabeth stood helplessly by as her home was ransacked. Her furniture and winter supplies were taken and her feather beds were ripped open and destroyed. Before the mob left, they pulled logs loose from the side of the house until the roof caved in. Near Albany, an anonymous loyalist wife and her children were "stript by the Rebels of every individual thing belonging to them," including money and clothing and supplies. In Albany, the mob was not content only to destroy one loyalist woman's home; they also beat her and her daughter severely.[3]

Stories of violence and destruction were repeated in western Pennsylvania and along the frontier of the Carolinas, where, like the wives of patriot soldiers, the wives of loyalist soldiers were left behind to manage as best they could. But because these women were part of a political minority, they often lacked the support of neighbors and friends when the mob attacked. Sometimes, even a woman's parents turned their backs on her. When Elizabeth Bowman's home on the Susquehanna River was plundered and her husband and oldest son taken prisoner, her mother and father refused to take her in. Left with little alternative, Elizabeth took her children and made her way to the Mohawk River. Here she joined a group of women who survived on the small crop of potatoes and corn they could produce. It was the British commander at Niagara who finally rescued Elizabeth and her companions, bringing the "five women and thirty one children" to the safety of the fort. The British were amazed to find only one pair of shoes in the group's possession. Mary Munro of Shaftsbury, Vermont, fared little better. When her husband left to join Burgoyne's army, Mary became "the prey of every person around." Fearful that she and her family would not survive, she pleaded with her soldier husband to rescue them. "Is there no possibility of your sending for us? If there is no method fallen upon we shall perish, for you have no idea of our sufferings here." When her husband did not act, Mary turned to her parents. But they offered nothing but reproaches and criticism. "My own relations," she wrote, "are my greatest enemies."[4]

When neighbors or family did help, they sometimes preferred to remain anonymous. Just before the Land family's home on the Delaware River in New Jersey was burned to the ground, a mysterious figure warned them to flee. Mr. Land was away, carrying dispatches for the British, but his wife and children gathered what they could and hurried into the woods. Eventually they made their way to the sanctuary of British-occupied New York City. None of the Lands could identity the person who had saved their lives.[5]

Many women chose to leave their communities rather than remain in the midst of their enemies. Simple flight was one option, but often this meant leaving home without any of their possessions and undertaking a long and arduous journey to Canada or Florida. The alternative, especially in

New England and New York, was to formally petition local patriot authorities for safe passage and permission to bring personal possessions and supplies into British territory. Even then, the price was high. The American officials set limits on what a woman could take with her and demanded that she pay all the costs incurred in traveling to British lines. She had to leave any son over the age of twelve behind to serve in the patriot army, and she was often forced to leave infants and small children behind as well, for they had little chance of surviving the arduous journey.

Although the requests for safe passage were straightforward, they posed a serious dilemma for American officials. If a petition were granted, the reunion of a loyalist soldier and his family might boost the man's morale and keep him in the British army. Even worse from the patriot perspective, the woman might prove to be a good source of intelligence for the British, supplying information on the size and location of the local patriot forces, news of troop movements, and the degree of support for the Revolution within her community. But refusing the petitions might cause other problems. A loyalist woman who remained in patriot territory could just as easily provide information to the enemy and shelter and supplies to loyalist or Indian raiding parties. In New Jersey, frustrated patriot officials appealed to Governor William Livingston to rid the New Ark community of a group of "Tory Women" whose activities had "impeaded their business." The twenty women named were accused of a variety of efforts to undermine the Revolution: "they Secret the goods & conceal everything they possible can from [us], which gives them a great deal of Trouble . . . have been great plunderers & concealers of goods, & when Called in for any thing, they petition to have Leave to go among Christians, & not be detain'd among Brutes as they call us in this Town. . . ." From the point of view of the local officials, sending these twenty women to their husbands who were serving in the enemy's military "will be an Advantage to the State, and save the Committion a Great deal of Trouble."[6]

Perhaps the biggest drawback to refusing a woman's petition was a simple economic one, for if she stayed, she and her children were likely to become a drain on the local community's resources. The mob might destroy her home, but local officials owed her assistance. The situation was ironic: the destruction of a loyalist woman's home and farm made her enemies responsible for her family's survival. Despite the very real cost of their decision, some patriot officials refused to allow loyalist wives and children a peaceful departure. At least one New York county tried to turn the situation to its advantage. There, officials attempted to use local loyalist women and children as bargaining chips. They would let the families go, they said, if the British would release certain prisoners of war in exchange. Their attempt at negotiation failed, however, for British military commanders and civil officers were no more eager to shoulder the burden of support "for a number of useless Consumers of Provisions" than the patriots.[7]

In the end, the issue proved moot, for the most desperate and the most determined women left without waiting for permission. Yet the debates over these petitions, like the occasional arrest and jailing of loyalist women convicted of spying or sheltering enemy troops, raised the issue of autonomous political commitment and action by women. Were intelligence gathering and provisioning the enemy, in other words, to be seen as simple acts of wifely loyalty, or were they evidence of independent political choices? As evidence mounted of loyalist women actively supporting the enemy government, officials were forced to acknowledge the possibility of autonomous political commitments by the enemy's wives and daughters. Thus statutes defining treason began to speak of "persons" rather than men, of "he and she" rather than "he" alone. When New York issued its Act of Attainder in 1779, three women—Margaret Inglis, Susannah Robinson, and Mary Morris—were named as traitors, their disloyalty to the Revolution declared a felony. In some cases, a woman suspected of aiding her loyalist husband or his military comrades—either by supplying information or by providing food and shelter to them—could be jailed and her children left to fend for themselves.

In Vermont, the revolutionary council specifically condemned loyalist women of their state who had been "riding post, carrying Intelligence to the Enemies Camp and Scouts" as "dangerous persons to Society and instruments of Great Mischief to this and the United States of America."[8]

So they could be—and were. Women not only openly resisted the demands of local patriot committees to submit to their authority, they also encouraged others to refuse to take the loyalty oath to the new governments. Others, like the three women who plotted to kidnap the mayor of Albany, and the woman who helped destroy a rebel town, were willing to engage in criminal acts. Most of the women who actively supported the Crown, however, chose to aid loyalist soldiers or gather vital information for the British. When Rachel Ferguson's sons joined the British army, for example, she and her daughters provided supplies and hiding places for British raiding parties. Other loyalist women hid their husbands from arrest by local committees. Still others hid important papers or money from the authorities. And one enterprising woman dressed a group of wounded loyalists and their Indian allies in women's clothing and nursed them back to health in her home, right under the eyes of un-suspecting, and apparently inattentive, patriots. British officers testified to the valuable role loyalist women like Hannah Tomlinson played "in assisting, & secreting our Troops (who had fallen into the Hands of the Enemy) that wished to escape from them & return to us." It was the fear that women could make political commitments and act on them, and the many instances in which they did, that accounts for the reprisals taken against them both by mobs and by Revolutionary officials.[9]

Where loyalist women went when they fled the Revolution was influenced by their social class, their region, and their husbands' wishes. Most wealthy loyalists, especially those who had held royal appointments in the colonies, settled for a time in England. And although some, like Joseph Galloway, left their wives behind to protect their property, many brought their families with them. Thus Esther Sewall dutifully followed her husband into exile, first in London and then in the less expensive English port city of Bristol. There she was subjected to Jonathan's increasingly mad ravings against a world that had cut short his career and sunk him into poverty. For almost eighteen months he locked himself in a room, and by the time he emerged from his self-imposed solitary confinement, he had convinced himself that Esther was responsible for the American Revolution. Although Nelly Boucher did not have to endure paranoid accusations from her husband, the Anglican minister and planter Jonathan Boucher, she did suffer from the sudden shift from rural Maryland to urban London. In his reminiscences, Jonathan recounts that Nelly asked him to pause on a London street until the crowd went by. The crowd, he told her gently, was simply the typical rush of Londoners and would never go by.[10]

Eventually, most of the loyalists who went to England made a second emigration to Canada. Here they found themselves among the thousands of ordinary loyalists, veterans and their families, widows and their children, who poured into Nova Scotia and Upper Canada. These men and women had sought refuge with the British army, had journeyed to safety behind British lines during the war, or had been evacuated by the British from ports like New York and Charleston when the war ended.

The earliest women refugees to Canada came from the borderlands of New York, Vermont, and New Hampshire, and most had harrowing tales of their flight. Traveling with newborn babies, sleeping in the woods, paddling canoes in the darkness along the rivers and across the lakes, they made their way to the forts and small communities that flew the British flag. The odyssey of Sarah Sherwood, the wife of loyalist officer Justus Sherwood, was typical. Seven months pregnant in 1777, Sarah began her journey with an American escort, her children, and a slave named Caesar Congo. The first leg of her trip was by wagon to Skenesborough. There, Sarah and her family took a bateau on Lake Champlain, headed for Ticonderoga. It was early November when they arrived, only to find the fort deserted. Her

American escort deposited her and her family thirty miles from the nearest British outpost—and then fled, afraid that the British might capture him. Sarah, carrying her infant daughter and leading her three-year-old son by the hand, began the long walk to the British fort at Pointe au Fer. Caesar Congo followed, carrying what supplies he could. From Pointe au Fer, the family took a second bateau to Fort St. Jean, on the Richelieu River. Here Sarah was reunited briefly with her husband and began her life in the shadow of the military. Ann Peters and her seven children had a similar experience. Traveling by sleigh in the dead of winter in 1777, they made the 140-mile trip to the American-held fort at Ticonderoga. Although nearly dead from the journey, they were only allowed to stay at the fort until the spring thaw. That April, the Americans gave Ann Peters three weeks' provisions and deposited her and her children many miles from British territory. For eighteen days, the Peters family waited until a British boat found them and carried them to Saint John's.[11]

Women like Sarah Sherwood and Ann Peters were as heroic as the women who defied patriot demands for loyalty oaths, sheltered loyalist soldiers, or gathered intelligence information for the British while they were still behind enemy lines. Yet, when they arrived in Canada or reached the safety of the British army, their boldness was often concealed by a mantle of modesty, their independence of mind by an acceptance of subordination. It was not difficult to understand this resort to feminine frailty: most of these women were totally dependent upon the charity and support of a hierarchy of male officers or government officials. It was this dependency that led husbands to speak of their wives as helpless and dependent when they applied to the Crown for relief, and it was this image that widows and daughters invoked when they sought continuing relief. Necessity had prompted them to perform acts of daring; now necessity kept them silent about their achievements.[12]

A steady flow of loyalists into Canada continued throughout the war, although the greatest number came in 1775 and 1783. In 1775, a thousand of the less prosperous New England loyalists boarded ships headed for Nova Scotia. And, in 1783, over seven thousand more loyalists, many of them veterans, camp followers, or widows, were evacuated from New York City. Although a small number were bound for Bermuda or Kingston, Jamaica, most were headed northward. When the emigration ended, almost fifty thousand exiles had begun new lives in Canada.

Few began those lives with optimism. As the 170 sailing vessels cleared Boston Harbor in 1775, a loyalist is said to have declared, "Neither Hell, Hull nor Halifax can afford worse shelter than Boston." But Sarah Frost, who sailed from New York to Canada with 250 other passengers crammed aboard the *Two Sisters*, would not have agreed. On her arrival in June 1783, she wrote in her diary that Canada was "the roughest land I ever saw." Sarah Frost's first impression was echoed by other refugees to Nova Scotia who dubbed it "Nova Scarcity." Saint John's, New Brunswick, was no better. "Of all the vile countries that ever were known," began a poem of the day, "In the frigid or torrid or temperate zone / From accounts I had there is not such another; / It neither belongs to this world nor the other." Many years after the war ended, a Canadian statesman recalled his grandmother's account of her arrival at Saint John's. "I climbed to the top of Chipman's Hill," she said, "and watched the sails disappear in the distance, and such a feeling of loneliness came over me that though I had not shed a tear through all the war, I sat down on the damp moss with my baby on my lap and cried bitterly."[13]

A longing for home and a general weariness permeated the writing of many loyalist women. But many expressed a stoic resignation and a longing for peacefulness that had clearly eluded men like Jonathan Sewall. When a Scottish American woman named Cameron prepared to leave her home in the Mohawk Valley for a life of exile, she told her friends:

At last we are preparing to leave forever this land of my birth . . . The long, weary years of war . . . are over. . . . Our lands are confiscated and it is hard to raise money at forced sales. . . . We expect the journey to be long and hard and cannot tell how many weeks we will be on the road . . . I love friendship and neighborly kindness and am so glad that there will be no more taunting among the elders, no more bickering among the children. Bitter feelings are gone forever. . . . When I leave this beautiful Mohawk Valley and the lands I had hoped we would always hold, I shall hear no more the words, "Tory and Parricide" . . . The March of the Cameron Men and wives and children must tread the hard road. . . .[14]

For loyalists of modest means, it did prove to be a hard road. Exile thrust most of these loyalists into the most primitive of conditions during their early months in Canada, with many families living in tents during bitterly cold winters until a crude cabin could be constructed. Mary Fisher, the wife of a soldier in the New Jersey Volunteers, recalled her first winter in New Brunswick when deep snow lay on the ground around the makeshift tents of the refugees. "How we lived through that awful winter I hardly know," she wrote. "There were mothers, that had been reared in a pleasant country enjoying all the comforts of life, with helpless children in their arms. They clasped their infants to their bosoms and tried by the warmth of their own bodies to protect them from the bitter cold." Hannah Ingraham recalled how happy her family was to settle into a house with no floor, no windows, no chimney, and no door. At least, she explained, it was a roof over their heads. And, humble though this first home was, Hannah's mother, like Mrs. Cameron, was grateful to be far away from the dangers of the war itself. As they sat down to eat a meal of toasted bread, she declared, "This is the sweetest meal I have tasted in many a day."[15]

Wealthier families fared better, of course. In Halifax, Nova Scotia, elite exiles labored to reconstitute the social world they had left behind. By 1780, Rebecca Byles, daughter of the Reverend Mather Byles of Boston, could boast that her family had "bought a large, convenient House, with a very good Garden, Yard, & every other convenience, & what I exceedingly value, live exactly opposite our Friends . . ." In 1783, Sarah Winslow could assure her friend Benjamin Marston that "balls and assemblys have begun," even if, she added, they took place amidst confusion and dust. And Penelope Winslow wrote to a friend in 1785 that "feasting, card playing & dancing is the great business of Life at Halifax . . ."[16]

Despite the patina of elegance, many of these same elite women conceded that Halifax was no match for the life they had enjoyed in British-occupied New York. That was true civilization when compared with "this ruder World." But it was less the rudeness of Canadian exile than the fact of exile itself that troubled these women. It was the separation from one's "Father, friend and Companion" that left Penelope Winslow in despair; it was the memory of the "tyranny of exulting enemys" that still rankled with Sarah Winslow. And it was the lost farms, lost occupations, lost possessions that continued to weigh on the minds of ordinary exiled women who could recount the exact number of horses, cattle, and hogs lost to "the Rebels." The Revolution had forced these women to "undertake & prosecute a jou[r]ney a Crosse ye wilderness," not simply a physical wilderness but a social one, into exile from family and friends, church and community, the sights and sounds of home.[17]

CHAPTER 7

"THE WOMEN MUST HEAR
OUR WORDS"

The Revolution in the Lives of Indian Women

W hile Esther Reed and Esther Sewall prepared for the profound changes in their lives that a war for American independence might bring, Indian women faced far different circumstances. For Native Americans, this war between mother country and colonies posed a diplomatic crisis: what alliance would benefit them as a third party to the dispute? Much was at stake. Most of the Iroquois, the Cherokee, and the Choctaw—the major confederations of the borderlands—believed that an alliance with the British held out the greatest hope of protecting their lands and sustaining essential trade with white society. An American victory might mean liberty and freedom for colonists, but it would surely mean an onslaught of land speculators and settlers into Indian territories and governments that backed unfavorable treaties with threats of military force. For Indian women, an American victory would have other tragic consequences: their social roles

151

would be dramatically changed and their power within their communities diminished. Beginning in 1776, a revolution did take place in their lives, but it was not the revolution Abigail Adams or Martha Washington would remember.

Much of Indian society remained inexplicable to English colonists, despite years of contact, trade, warfare, diplomacy, and missionary work. In politics and in trade these two very different societies managed to operate on a "middle ground," which might best be described as a zone of cultural compromise rather than an actual physical location.[1] Here, a political vocabulary developed that drew upon both Indian customs and white ones, and here judgment was suspended so that goods could flow between the two societies. But in matters of gender roles, there could be no compromise and no suspension of judgment: everything about the gender arrangements of most Iroquois or Cherokee communities seemed to the English to be, in a word, wrong.

Indian cultures were as diverse as European, of course. Even among the Eastern Woodland Indians, variations of language, religious beliefs and practices, economic organization, and political structures were as common as among the French, English, or Dutch. But, just as in Europe, a common gendered division of labor did exist, especially among those Indian groups engaged in agriculture: a man hunted and a woman farmed.

152

To the English colonists, this division of labor defied all they knew to be true of male and female aptitudes and appropriate roles. In their society, masculinity was synonymous with the field and the plow; femininity, with the household and the hearth. Far more disturbing to these Englishmen and -women was the power that women wielded, especially in Indian societies that relied primarily upon agriculture. Many of these societies were matrilineal, tracing their family lines through the mother rather than the father. To women and men raised in a world where social and legal legitimacy was defined by the father, this was shocking. Even more puzzling to the colonists were the matrilocal traditions by which married couples or a woman and her children lived with her mother's family. Without a household of his own, a father's dominion over his family could not be established. Perhaps most disturbing of all was the public voice Indian women enjoyed in matters of war and peace. Among the Iroquois, clan mothers chose the tribal chiefs and had the power to remove them if they saw fit. Women councillors, present at formal discussions of war and diplomacy, had a powerful voice, able to block a decision if they believed it threatened their kin. As one Oneida chief tried to explain to white diplomats: "It was always the custom for [women] to be present [at councils], being of much estimation among us, in that we proceed from them, & they provide our Warriors with provisions when they go abroad."

For those steeped in the English traditions of the subordination of women, women's councils and women warriors were a radical crossing of gender lines. Even Sir William Johnson, long the superintendent of Indian affairs in the Mohawk Valley and a man who understood and appreciated Iroquois tradition, resisted women's active role in negotiations. Thus, when colonists thought about Indians at all—and by the 1770s, this was increasingly rare in the seaport towns and long-settled regions where native populations had been eradicated or subdued and segregated—Indian society seemed to mock the laws of God and Nature.[2]

There are few records of Indian women's view of English colonial society. Those that exist suggest amazement at the female dependency and exclusion from political life that marked a culture that was as alien to them as theirs was to the English. Ironically, the Indian perspective is often most vividly recorded in the memoirs of white women captured in raids on English settlements who chose to remain with the Indian tribes that adopted them. Mary Jemison, for example, describes the pleasures of collective work in the fields with Seneca women and girls, a contrast to the solitary housework she envisioned as a proper colonial matron. Not all captives preferred Indian society, of course; the seventeenth century's most famous captive, Mary Rowlandson, wrote with contempt of the Wampanoag woman warrior who held her prisoner, describing her as vain and proud and wholly lacking in the mercy and gentleness that defined a civilized woman.[3]

The individual Indian women of the Revolutionary era whose lives are known to us, women like Molly Brant or Nancy Ward, reveal their efforts to coexist with the white society around them. After the American Revolution, the terms of that coexistence were set entirely by the white victors. Thus the Revolution sparked a conquest, not only of Indian territories but of Indian cultures, as the Americans imposed their gender roles upon Indians who remained within their boundaries.

Molly Brant's life bridged two worlds.[4] She was born a Mohawk Indian, into a family that practiced an Iroquois form of Christianity and sent her to be educated in a white school. In 1759, at the age of sixteen, she married a widower, Sir William Johnson. Theirs was a match of equals, not in age but in status, for she was the daughter of one chief and the sister of another while he was the British Crown's northern superintendent of Indian affairs. They each wielded considerable influence in their own worlds. William was a wealthy New York landowner; Molly was a member of the Iroquois women's Society of Six Nations Matrons. Yet each stepped with considerable ease into the other's native world. Molly became the gracious hostess of the Johnson manor house;

William practiced many of the Iroquois rituals as Warraghiyageh ("he who has charge of affairs"), the adopted brother of the Mohawks. Together, Molly and William became the most powerful political force in the Mohawk Valley, creating and sustaining links to both the white and the Indian societies around them. For twenty-two years, Molly and Sir William represented the possibility of peaceful coexistence and mutual respect between the two races. While Britain ruled the colonies, Molly Brant's two worlds, the white and the Indian, seemed to be in harmony.

The American Revolution shattered that harmony and effectively ended the power that Molly's Iroquois kinsmen and -women had wielded for almost two centuries. Since the seventeenth century, the English and French governments had courted the great Indian confederacies of the North and South, hoping that alliances with them would tip the balance of power in favor of their own imperial ambitions. For their part, Iroquois, Creek, and Choctaw leaders used the fierce imperial rivalries of the Europeans to gain advantages in trade and secure their territory against encroachment. The Indians' power to play one European suitor against another began to vanish in the 1760s, however. The victory of the English in the French and Indian Wars left the Iroquois of the northern region with no alternative but to negotiate an alliance with the British Crown. To the South, Choctaw and Creek now relied more heavily upon the British government to stem the tide of colonial settlers into their homelands. As the tensions between colonists and Crown deepened, Indians like Molly Brant were caught up in the crisis of loyalties.

In the early 1770s, neither Indian nor Englishman could foresee the impact of the growing tensions between patriots and Crown upon these great confederacies. In the beginning, the balance of power seemed to be with the Indians, for patriots, loyalists, and the British government all courted them. Uncertain where their advantage lay, the Six Nations of the Iroquois gathered in council in October 1774. Under the leadership of Molly Brant's brother, the young Mohawk chief Joseph Thayendanegea—or as the English knew him, Joseph Brant—the Iroquois declared their determination to remain at peace with both the Crown and the colonists. The quarrel, they said, was between brothers; they had no reason to become involved.

Yet, as the war began, the pressures from all sides increased. Americans, who doubted their ability to win an alliance with the Six Nations, bargained hard for continuing neutrality among these northern tribes. The Continental Congress reinforced the notion of the war as an internal dispute among Englishmen, calling it "a quarrel between us and Old England" that should not concern the Indians. The British, on the other hand, declared themselves the true heirs of the "covenant chain," an alliance forged between the English king and the Iroquois in the 1760s, and pressed for a commitment of men and supplies.

By 1778, the unity of the Iroquois Six Nations had been shattered by a choice of loyalties. Most of the Mohawks, Onondagas, Cayugas, and Seneca took up arms for the British while the Oneidas and the Tuscaroras fought on the side of the rebellion. To a great extent, the choices made by the Iroquois tribes hinged on an assessment of the practical benefits from an alliance; but there were other factors at play. The Oneidas and Tuscaroras were drawn to the American cause by their attachment to New England missionaries like Samuel Kirkland; the Mohawks were drawn to the British by their long attachment to Sir William Johnson. Although Johnson had died in 1774, his widow, Molly Brant, kept those ties strong during the long war between king and colonists. In the South, both the Cherokee and the Choctaw cast their lot with the British in an effort to stop, or at least slow down, the movement of land-hungry American settlers into their territories. A deep hatred of colonial expansion fueled their decision.

When the first shots were fired at Lexington and Concord, Molly was a forty-year-old widow, living at the manor house with her children and stepchildren. Both American and English authorities understood how valuable she could be in any negotiation with the Iroquois. As Lieutenant Colonel Tench Tilghman, the secretary to the

American Indian Commissioners, crassly put it, "Women govern the Politics of savages." A clever man, he added, "always kept up a good understanding with the brown ladies. . . ." But the Americans could not reach an understanding with this particular brown lady. From the beginning, Molly was a loyalist. She believed her political commitment to the Crown honored her husband's memory and, most importantly, served the best interest of her Mohawk kinsmen and -women. Yet, despite her vocal opposition to the Revolution and the rising patriot fever around her, Molly also believed that her roots in both the white and Indian worlds would protect her from harm. Events soon proved her wrong.[5]

In 1777 Molly's loyalism became a matter of deeds as well as words. As the British were laying siege to the American-held Fort Stanwix, Molly learned that a neighbor was leading a band of local patriots to reinforce the beleaguered American troops. She immediately sent word to Mohawk and loyalist troops under the command of her brother, Joseph Brant, who ambushed the Americans at the Oriskany ravines. Molly's role in this Oriskany attack placed her in danger from both local patriots and the Oneida Indians, who had recently cast their lot with the revolutionaries. Settlers in the valley refused to sell her needed supplies; Oneidas took her livestock and killed her overseer. Together, a patriot and Oneida raiding party entered her home and destroyed most of her possessions. Accepting at last that her family was in danger, Molly Brant fled the manor house for the safety of a nearby Cayuga village.

After General Burgoyne's defeat at Saratoga, Molly was persuaded to move once again, this time to safety behind British lines. In her flight, she had been able to take nothing of value with her; she arrived at Fort Niagara with little to remind her of her years as the mistress of an elegant manor house. Bitter at what she considered the betrayal of the Oneida and angered by the hostility of her white neighbors, Molly devoted herself to securing a British victory. As both the widow of Warraghiyageh and an Iroquois matron, she proved far more effective than the new superintendent of Indian affairs in rallying and sustaining the support of the Iroquois.

Throughout the war, the British relied heavily on Molly's influence with the Mohawks. It was Molly who persuaded the Society of Six Nations Matrons to press their men to fight for the king, and it was Molly who rallied these Indian warriors when they began to question their participation in the war. British officials never underestimated her importance. An officer at Carleton Island grudgingly conceded that the "good behavior" of the Indian refugees there "is in a great Measure to be ascribed to Miss Molly." Sir William Johnson's son-in-law, Daniel Claus, put it more bluntly: "A Joseph and Mary [Molly] Brant will outdo fifty [British officers] in managing and keeping the Indians firm. One word from Mary Brant is more taken notice of by the Five Nations than a thousand from the white man without exception."[6]

Molly used her influence to help her own people as well as the British cause. She skillfully interceded when clashes developed between Mohawks and the new superintendent of Indian affairs. Writing to Daniel Claus, she diplomatically reminded him that "the Indians are a good deal dissatisfied on account of [the superintendent's] hasty temper which I hope he will soon drop. Otherwise it may be disadvantageous. I need not tell you that whatever he promised or told them ought to be performed."[7]

As the war continued, Molly found herself living once again in two worlds, Indian and white. Like her, her son George was educated in white schools; like her, her daughter Elizabeth married a white man. But her identification with her Indian community remained strong, and when George took up arms against the rebels, he did so as part of Chief Joseph Brant's Mohawk troops. When the war ended in British defeat, Molly and her family settled on the Canadian lands given to them as compensation for their loyalty. Although her loyalty had been rewarded, she was an exile from her homeland.

For the remaining thirteen years of her life, Molly continued to serve as a vital link between the British and the Indians. She used her influence to prevent Mohawk military alliances with those Iroquois who remained in United States territories, and she worked to protect the lands granted to her own people by the Crown. When she died in April 1796, the bell in the tower of the local Anglican church at Cataraqui tolled for her, calling together merchants and political leaders, British officers from nearby Fort Frontenac, Mississauga chiefs, and Mohawk neighbors to mourn for her. Who would replace her? asked the Anglican minister from the church pulpit. It was a rhetorical question that both whites and Indians knew had no answer.

Although Molly Brant was the most powerful Indian woman of her generation, she was not the only Indian woman to lead rather than follow the men of her society. Among the Cherokee, Nanyehi, or Nancy Ward, was both a warrior and a diplomat.[8] Born in 1738 at Chota, the sacred town of the Cherokee, Nanyehi ("one who goes about") was the daughter of Tame Doe of the Wolf Clan and the niece of Attakullakulla, the civil chief of the Cherokee. She married Kingfisher, and by the time she was seventeen, she was the mother of two children, Five Killer and Catherine. In 1755, Nanyehi fought beside her husband in the battle of Taliwa, one of the many confrontations between the Cherokee and the Creeks during that decade. When Kingfisher was killed in battle, the eighteen-year-old Nanyehi is said to have rallied the Cherokee to victory. For her bravery, she was named a Ghighua, or "Beloved Woman," a title that honored women warriors or the wives and mothers of male warriors. With the title of Beloved Woman came a leadership role in the Cherokee nation. Nanyehi sat in the General Council, headed the Women's Council, participated in religious ceremonies, and served as a negotiator when treaties were made.

Her influence came at a time of increasing tension between whites and Cherokee, for settlers continually ignored the British government's policy against further incursions into Indian territories. While other Cherokee advocated violence against the white settlers, Nanyehi urged restraint, pressing for some compromise between white and Indian interests. Perhaps her marriage in the 1750s to the white trader Bryant Ward made her more hopeful that peaceful relationships could be established between Indians and whites. It was this that she worked for, and on several occasions, she warned the white families in the Watauga settlements of impending attacks. She even rescued one captive from death. The grateful woman, Lydia Bean, shared her housewifely skills with Nanyehi and other Cherokee women, teaching them to spin thread and weave cloth and to make dairy products such as butter and cream.

Throughout the Revolution, Nanyehi counseled compromise with the Americans while other

Cherokee leaders counseled war. At the 1781 negotiations that followed a series of attacks by Americans on Cherokee towns, Nanyehi pleaded for peace between the women of the two societies. But the negotiations demonstrated the great gulf between the place of women in Indian and white societies. When the terms of the treaty were agreed to, Nanyehi instructed John Sevier to take them back to the women of his tribe for ratification, for, she said, "the women must hear our words." Sevier was dumbstruck; in his world, women played no role in political and diplomatic affairs. Nanyehi was equally appalled; how could a treaty be signed if the women of Sevier's world did not give their consent?[9]

Like Molly Brant and Nanyehi, Queen Esther Montour wielded power among her people, the Munsee Delawares.[10] Esther's physical appearance reflected the many marriages between Europeans and Iroquois from which she descended. She was, a white settler recalled, "a tall, but not very fleshy woman—not as dark as the usual Indian in complexion—had the features of a white woman—cheek bones not high, hair black, but soft and fine like a white woman's . . . her form erect and commanding, her appearance and manners agreeable." Although her first husband was a Munsee Delaware chief, Esther was a Christian. And although it was the English who bestowed upon her the title of queen, it was the Delaware who made her the leader of the Munsees when her husband died.

By 1778, western New York and Queen Esther's own northern Pennsylvania were in flames, the scene of violent conflict between Indians and white settlers. For almost a year, the Indian and loyalist forces here held the upper hand, with troops under Joseph Brant burning the white settlement at Cobleskill, New York, to the ground that year. After Cobleskill, Brant and his men moved through Ulster County, terrorizing the patriot population there. Meanwhile, another large force of Iroquois and loyalists, led by John Butler and Cornplanter, headed toward Pennsylvania's Wyoming Valley. That summer, they seized several forts and Cornplanter's triumphant army burned and looted homes, destroyed mills, and drove off livestock.

Americans spoke bitterly of this destruction as the Wyoming Valley Massacre. Rumors soon spread and the tales of atrocities grew. Stories of Joseph Brant scalping innocent children were told and believed—although Brant was nowhere near the valley at the time. A similar tale was spread of Queen Esther, who allegedly sang a wild tune while she tomahawked over a dozen victims. Later, she was said to have bragged about her murder spree. The image of a heartless woman warrior, singing as she slaughtered, transformed Queen Esther into "Crazy Esther."

Neither Esther Montour nor any other woman

actually took part in the events of July 1778. But it is telling that white society continued to believe that "Crazy Esther" had butchered her neighbors. So much of Indian culture seemed to defy English norms that anything seemed possible to many white Americans. But Esther Montour was neither crazy nor bloodthirsty. Nor was she able to stem the tide of white incursions into her homeland. The Indian and loyalist victories in the Wyoming Valley prompted the Americans to mount a major western offensive. Under General John Sullivan, they adopted a slash-and-burn policy, destroying every Indian village they conquered. Queen Esther's own town of Tioga was among those Sullivan decimated.

A Seneca woman, Mary Jemison, left one of the most vivid accounts of the destruction Sullivan and his army wreaked among the northwestern Indian tribes.[11] Jemison, like Queen Esther and Molly Brant, knew what life was like in the two worlds of white and Indian society. Born into a white family, she had been taken captive in a Seneca raid when she was fifteen years old. When the opportunity came for her to be ransomed and returned to her New England home, Jemison refused. She found life as a wife and mother among the Seneca more attractive than the life awaiting her in colonial society. In the fall of 1779, as news came that Sullivan's army was approaching, the women and children of Mary's village were sent to safety in the woods. She recalled her flight, with "three children who went with me on foot, one who rode on horse back, and one whom I carried on my back." When the American army marched away, Mary and her companions returned to their village, only to find that Sullivan and his army had "destroyed every article of the food kind that they could lay their hands on. A part of our corn they burnt, and threw the remainder into the river. They burnt our houses, killed what few cattle and horses they could find, destroyed our fruit trees, and left nothing but the bare soil and timber." There was "not a mouthful of any kind of sustenance left, not even enough to keep a child one day from perishing of hunger."

As winter set in, Mary resolved to take her children away from the sad remains of their home. She walked with them, she wrote, until, at Gardeau Flats, she encountered "two negroes, who had run away from their masters sometime before." The men took Jemison and her family in, offering them food and shelter if she would help them harvest their corn. "I have laughed a thousand times to myself," Jemison later wrote, "when I have thought of the good old Negro, who hired me, who fearing that I should get taken or injured by the Indians, stood by me constantly when I was husking, with a loaded gun in his hand, in order to keep off the enemy, and thereby lost as much labor of his own as he received from me. . . ." In the eyes of these two men, Jemison was a white woman in need of protection from hostile Indians; in Jemison's eyes, she was a

Seneca, saddened by the fact that "many of our people barely escaped with their lives, and some actually died of hunger and freezing" because of the American army.

Molly Brant, Queen Esther, and Nancy Ward had no counterparts in colonial American society. The authority and autonomy that women enjoyed in their Indian societies stood in stark contrast to the accepted subordination and economic dependency of colonial farmwives or urban mothers. In white culture there was no society of matrons able to directly influence military and political decision making; there were no women's councils to decide the fate of treaties or of prisoners of war. Although ministers and political leaders in the colonies often described life among the Indians as a savage and degrading existence for women, there were white women like Mary Jemison who recorded that this was not so.

Yet the power of women within the Indian world was fading, and after the war, the cultural norms of the white world would soon be pressed upon the Iroquois and the Cherokee. Male leaders like Handsome Lake of the Seneca would urge his people to re-create their families and communities in the English image in order to survive. As agriculture became the domain of Indian men, as it was of white men, the economic power of Indian women began to vanish. And as Christianity became the religion of many Indian communities and traditional rituals that required women's participation were abandoned, the spiritual role of women would be diminished. Nanyehi could not have known that the skills she learned from Lydia Bean would become part of a repertoire of household skills that would define—and confine— Indian women to the "small circle of domestic concerns" in which white women operated.

Indian women's political voice was rarely acknowledged by American governments, and thus women's power and authority waned. By the early nineteenth century, Cherokee women no longer negotiated treaties as Nanyehi had once done. Instead, like white American women, their only political tactic was the petition. In 1817, "the Cherokee ladys," acting out of a sense of "their duty as mothers," petitioned the male chiefs and warriors of their community not to sell any more land to white settlers. "Your mothers, your sisters ask and beg of you," they wrote, in a humble manner that Beloved Women would not have recognized as their own.[12]

CHAPTER 8

"THE DAY OF JUBILEE IS COME"

African American Women and the American Revolution

Molly Brant and Thomas Jefferson shared a desire for freedom and independence—and went to war with each other to ensure that these ideals became reality. The same dream of freedom motivated African American women and their families to wage their own war against those who enslaved them. In the struggle that Joseph Brant called a war between English "brothers," African American loyalties were to their own future, not to Congress or to king.

While leading patriots decried the king's efforts to enslave his American subjects, African American slavery was an accepted social institution in every American colony. Black slaves could be found working in shops in Boston, on the docks of New York City, in the elegant homes of Philadelphia's merchant elite, in the tobacco fields of Virginia, and in the rice paddies of South Carolina. By 1770, there were more than 47,000 enslaved blacks in the northern colonies, almost 20,000 of them in New York. More than 320,000 slaves worked the tobacco and wheat fields of the Chesapeake colonies, making 37 percent of the population of the region African or African American. More than 187,000 of these slaves were Virginians. In the Lower South, more than 92,000 slaves could be found wading deep in the putrid waters of the rice paddies or laboring at trades in the cities of Charleston or Savannah. South Carolina alone had more than 75,000 slaves, and by 1770 planters there were importing 4,000 more Africans a year. More than a third of the thriving plantations of the Lower South boasted slave populations of fifty or more, so that in many counties the black population far outnumbered the white. Although free black women and men could also be found in every colony, the trend toward emancipation had slowed greatly by the middle of the eighteenth century. In New York, Pennsylvania, and New England, colonial governments had placed obstacles in the way of any master wishing to free his slaves.[1]

No matter where they lived, slaves endured hard and demeaning lives. But labor in the southern colonies was most severe. Tobacco production, done by gang labor, was both tedious and demanding, but rice production was, as one observer declared, "I think the hardest work I have seen [slaves] engage in."[2] On the whole, slaves were poorly fed and poorly clothed, and subject to both physical and psychological abuse. From humiliating names to humiliating punishments, slaves learned the meaning of freedom every day by its absence.

Whether slave or free, African American women struggled to establish and maintain a family. Free black women who worked as household servants were usually not allowed to set up an independent household with a husband or children. Enslaved black women working in northern households were often sold away when they became pregnant, separating them from their husbands and relatives. On the plantations of the Chesapeake, slave gangs were usually housed at a distance from other gangs, and frequently their members were segregated by age or sex. Husbands and wives who lived on different plantations had even greater difficulty keeping up their relationships. And as planters opened up new lands in the Piedmont regions and further west, families were split apart. In every southern colony, the death of a master or the marriage of a master's child could mean a black family divided, for widows rented out slaves and fathers gave slaves to their daughters as wedding gifts. Planters often put young slave boys up for sale, separating them from their parents, or sold family members as punishment for insolence or bad work habits.[3]

Throughout the colonial period, enslaved people had made their bids for freedom, either in groups or as solitary runaways. On plantations that bordered Spanish, French, or Indian territory, or in areas where an escape to a busy port city was possible, runaways had some chance of finding refuge or melting into the crowds. Most runaways, however, were male. Pregnant women, mothers with infants and small children, and women who cared for elderly parents or friends, could not—and would not—abandon those who depended upon them.

The year 1775 brought new possibilities to slave and free women in every colony. The emerging conflict between mother country and colonies led loyalists, British officials, army commanders, and patriots to appeal to African Americans for support. The near-constant presence of British armies in the Lower South, the American army's desperate need for soldiers and laborers, and recruitment by guerrilla loyalist and patriot bands in the southern backcountry all created opportunities for black women as well as men to escape slavery. The disruption of daily life, the chaos and confusion that marked the war in the South, the flight of masters and their families to safer ground—these realities, more than any broadening of the meaning of "freedom" embraced by patriots, allowed tens of thousands of African Americans to enjoy small blessings of liberty at last.

The British were certainly the first to recognize the potential benefits of an alliance between the Crown and the enslaved. On November 7,

1775, with the colonies on the verge of revolution, the governor of Virginia, the Earl of Dunmore, issued a proclamation that terrified white plantation owners and brought hope to their slaves. As a "Body of . . . Traitors, and their Abettors" threatened to attack the king's troops in Virginia, Dunmore declared "all indented Servants, Negroes, or others . . . free that are able and willing to bear Arms, they joining his MAJESTY'S Troops as soon as may be. . . ." Dunmore assumed, rightly, that many black men would be willing to fight against their masters. He also hoped that the loss of slave labor would be an economic blow to the rebels. As the war progressed, both proved to be true: black soldiers would fight side by side with British regulars, in their own black regiments, and in Hessian regiments, and an estimated 80,000 to 100,000 African Americans, both male and female, would desert their masters before the war ended, damaging the tobacco economy of the Chesapeake and leaving the plantation economy of the Carolinas in ruins.[4]

By December 1, some three hundred runaway male slaves had enlisted in what Dunmore called his Ethiopian Regiment. Across their chests, these men wore a banner that read "Liberty to Slaves." With them came women and children, hoping that Dunmore's protection would extend to them as well. To counter the effect of Dunmore's proclamation, the Virginia Committee of Safety issued a warning to the colony's slaves: "To none is freedom promised but to such as are able to do Lord Dunmore's service: The aged, the infirm, the women and children, are still to remain the property of their masters." What would become of those left behind? The committee's answer was a chilling threat: "masters . . . will be provoked to severity, should part of their slaves desert them . . . should there be any amongst the Negroes weak enough to believe that Dunmore intends to do them a kindness, and wicked enough to provoke the fury of the Americans against their defenceless fathers and mothers, their wives, their women and children, let them only consider the difficulty of effecting their escape, and what they must expect to suffer if they fall into the hands of the Americans."[5]

Dunmore's biracial army could not withstand the force of Virginia's rebels, however. It was defeated outside Norfolk, and the governor fled to British ships waiting in the Chesapeake. He took the surviving members of the Ethiopian Regiment and other black refugees aboard with him. But worse was to follow. A smallpox epidemic broke out on board the ships, and Dunmore, hoping to contain it, ordered the African Americans to be isolated on an island in the bay. Later, when the Americans took the island, they found "many poor Negroes . . . dying of the putrid fever; others dead in the open fields; a child was found sucking at the breast of its dead mother." Before the disease ran its course, half the Ethiopian Regiment had died.[6]

Virginia planters moved quickly to prevent any further loss of slaves to the British. Virginia's patriot leadership threatened death or resale to the West Indies to "all Negro or other Slaves, conspiring to rebel or make insurrection," and to make their point, they sold thirty-two of the Ethiopian Regiment soldiers they had captured in battle to planters in the Caribbean. Threats like these did not prevent the flight of some five thousand African Americans from Virginia and the surrounding Chesapeake region during the course of the war. But the British army would not be there to shelter them. The war moved out of Virginia before independence was declared, and did not return until General Cornwallis made his last stand at Yorktown in 1781.[7]

The greatest push for self-emancipation came in the Lower South, the scene of brutal civil war and two major British military campaigns. Slave women, like slave men, took advantage of the violent confusion to seek safety behind British lines. Some British commanders were willing to arm able-bodied black men, but the majority of male and female refugees were set to work making musket cartridges, tending to the sick and wounded in hospitals, or performing the backbreaking labor of building fortifications and repairing roads. Not a few were assigned to work as personal servants for British officers.

Despite all the difficulties and dangers, wherever the British army went in the South, black men and women followed in its wake. The number of runaways increased dramatically after June 1779 when the British commander, Sir Henry Clinton, issued a second proclamation, known as the Philipsburg Proclamation. In it, General Clinton declared that "every NEGRO who shall desert the Rebel Standard" would be granted "full security to follow within these Lines, any Occupation which he shall think proper." Although Clinton intended the proclamation to encourage African Americans serving in the Continental Army to desert, thousands of civilian blacks read it as a general promise of emancipation. Men, women, and children poured into the British camps. Others, taking advantage of the confusion and chaos that the war in the South produced, made their escape to Maroon communities in Florida or on the borderlands of Carolina and Georgia.[8]

When Cornwallis's army moved north from the Carolinas to Virginia in 1781, over four thousand black men and women trailed behind the baggage carts. Dianah and Hannah of the Linning plantation were perhaps typical of the women who chose to run away. Before the Revolution, escape would have been impossible for this elderly woman and her half-blind daughter. But when the British army crossed the Linning fields on their way to Charleston, Dianah and Hannah went with them.

When the British surrendered Charleston to the American army, mother and daughter sailed with them to New York and from there, at last, to freedom in Canada aboard the British transport ship *Elijah*.[9]

Although Dianah and Hannah made it safely to Canada when the loyalists were finally evacuated from New York, the majority of slaves who sought their freedom did not. Half of the women and men who answered the call issued in Clinton's Philipsburg Proclamation did not survive the war. And despite the proclamation's promise, many who survived were not allowed their freedom. Both loyalists and British regulars considered them, like the slaves captured on American plantations, to be prizes of war.

Even official documents of emancipation sometimes failed to protect African Americans. In Charleston, for example, a loyalist named Jesse Gray made a career of false claims of ownership and the resale of emancipated blacks. Mary Postill was one of his victims. Postill was the slave of a wealthy South Carolina planter who fled with her children to British-held Charleston. Here the military gave her a certificate of freedom. When the American army reclaimed Charleston in 1782, Mary, her husband, and her family went to St. Augustine, Florida, as the hired servants of Jesse Gray. But Gray had managed to take Postill's certificate and now declared that she and her family were legally his slaves. Soon after they arrived in St. Augustine, Jesse Gray sold Mary Postill to his brother Samuel. When the Gray brothers emigrated to Canada, they took Mary and her daughters with them. In Canada, Samuel Gray sold Mary Postill back to his brother. Fearful that Jesse Gray would sell her once again, this time separating her from her children, Mary took her daughters and fled the Gray household. Gray went to court to recover her. Although Postill swore in court that she was a free woman when she left Charleston, Gray won his suit. To punish Postill, he took her down the river and sold her to another loyalist for one hundred bushels of potatoes.[10]

As the war in the South turned in the Americans' favor, retreating British troops left many blacks behind. Most of these were re-enslaved. Left behind, too, were the enslaved women and men who had chosen not to leave their plantation homes. Few records exist to tell us why the majority of African American slave women did not flee. Some may have feared for the safety of their children in the midst of battlefields and disease-ridden camps. Others may have feared reprisals if they were captured or returned to their masters. For many, the desire to be in familiar surroundings and among friends and family in a time of chaos and violence kept them at home.

Remaining home did not ensure a woman's safety or secure the well-being of her family, however. Ironically, the flight of so many others

left them vulnerable. On South Carolina plantations, where desertions ran high, there were not
enough field hands to plant or harvest crops. Food
grew scarce, and it was "the poor Negroes" who
remained behind who starved. Wartime decisions
made by planters harmed them as well. Slave
owners hoping to protect their human property
from confiscation or theft chose to send their
slaves to places of safety like Florida, Louisiana,
or the West Indies, where they could be kept until
peace returned. If plantation owners chose to flee
themselves, they were rarely willing or able to take
all members of a slave family with them. Black
parents were thus separated from their children
and wives from their husbands. Slaves who
remained on rebel plantations also fared badly
when British troops seized their masters' possessions, for the soldiers considered them to be spoils
of war. In an effort to prevent individual soldiers
from claiming these slaves as personal property,
General Henry Clinton ordered that they be
treated as British property. His efforts were not
always effective, however, for soldiers learned to
quickly sell the captured slaves before officers
could intervene. This wartime trafficking in slaves,
observed South Carolina patriot Henry Laurens,
condemned African Americans to a "ten fold
worse slavery in the West Indies."[11]

Perhaps twenty thousand fugitive slaves left
the Lower South when the British abandoned
Savannah and Charleston at war's end. Along with

other loyalists, most were taken to New York City, where the final evacuation of British forces and their supporters was to take place. Even here, however, freedom was not final. Loyalist masters rushed to reclaim former slaves from among the refugee groups and patriot masters demanded the return of runaways. As preparations got under way, a rumor spread that the British intended to turn over all former slaves to their owners. "This dreadful rumour," recalled a black man, "filled us all with inexpressible anguish and terror, especially when we saw our old masters coming from Virginia, North Carolina, and other parts, and seizing their slaves in the streets of New York, or even dragging them out of their beds." Among those who were reclaimed by their masters were a "man, his wife, and a kinswoman of theirs," who had served the Baroness Riedesel during the years her family spent as prisoners of war in America. "They had served us faithfully," wrote the baroness, while their former master had "treated them shockingly." She remembered vividly the "shrieks and lamentations of these poor people" as they were taken away.[12]

Despite the successes of some slaveholders in reclaiming their human property, the worst fears of the refugees in New York proved unfounded. The British refused to turn blacks over to their former masters wholesale, although they did allow loyalists to bring their slaves with them as they boarded the ships for Canada. The British ultimately issued certificates of manumission to more than 1,300 men, 914 women, and 740 children as a reward for their wartime services. Their names, along with the names of slaves belonging to white loyalists, were recorded in a log known as *The Book of Negroes,* which contained a description of each person. To guard against ship captains putting free black loyalists in irons and carrying them to the West Indies for sale, *The Book of Negroes* also recorded the name of the ship they boarded, the name of the captain, and the official port of destination.[13]

On evacuation day, November 25, 1783, British transport ships began their journeys to Nova Scotia, New Brunswick, and the Caribbean. Each passenger list contained a sliver of the histories of African American freedom and bondage: for example, the Spring, headed for Saint John's, carried Ann Black, a twenty-five-year-old woman, and Sukey, a five-year-old girl, both free. Twenty-year-old Rose Richards, described as a "healthy young woman," was aboard the *Aurora,* traveling to Canada as the property of a white Philadelphia loyalist. On the same ship was Barbarry Allen, a "healthy stout wench" of twenty-two, who was the property of a Virginian, and twenty-four-year-old Elizabeth Black, a free mulatto woman. The *Ariel* carried thirty-two-year-old Betsy Brothers, traveling with two children and a certificate of manumission; thirty-year-old Dinah Mitchell, a "stout healthy Negress" with a child in her arms who had been freed by her master; and twenty-year-old Clara, a "stout wench," once the property of a Colonel De Bois, but left behind by him. The *Spencer* carried several emancipated women, including twenty-one-year-old Sarah Fox, a "stout healthy wench" who had somehow managed to purchase her freedom; the "stout little woman" Phebe Lynch, forty-two, once owned by a Mr. Lynch of South Carolina but now holding a certificate declaring her free; and young Hagar Corie, with her small child, once slaves on Great Neck, Long Island. On the *Peggy,* bound for Port Roseway, were Major Coffin's slave, the twenty-one-year-old Phebe, listed like so many other black women as a "stout wench"; and twenty-six-year-old Lettie, whose certificate showed her to be a freeborn woman from Montserrat. The *Peggy* also carried a young woman named Mary, listed as the property of her husband Joe, who "owned himself."

In Canada, former slaves were indeed free, but prejudice and poverty replaced their earlier bondage. The free black loyalists taken to Canada were segregated into black settlements like Little Tracadie and Brindley Town. The largest of these towns, Birchtown, was named in honor of the British general who authorized the certificates of manumission. Here, some 2,500 refugees began their new lives as free women and men. But whatever their hopes, few were realized. A racial as well as a class hierarchy determined the rations provided in the first years of settlement, with white officers and gentlemen served first, white veterans and working people next, and African Americans last of all. Of 649 male heads of household in Birchtown in 1784, only 184 had received the land grants promised to them by the Crown. White settlers, unhappy with their allotments, soon discovered means to deprive Birchtown residents of what land they did receive. The Anglican Church took property to the east of the settlement, and white settlers snatched up farmland to the north, carving lots out of the more valuable property surrounding the harbor.[14]

Conditions were little better in the smaller settlements. Sharecropping developed in some areas where whites had received large land grants they could not cultivate on their own. Many desperate blacks, giving up all hope of farmland, flocked to cities like Halifax, where low-paying jobs could be found. Even here, they found no peace. In 1784, poor white veterans in Shelburne rioted against blacks, whom they accused of forcing them out of the labor market. Black men and women were beaten, homes were destroyed, and many were forced to take refuge in nearby Birchtown. Landless and jobless women and men indentured themselves to white settlers or were sold as servants as punishment for vagrancy. Sometimes the motives for acts of violence were not economic but social. When a black Birchtown Baptist minister, David George, began to baptize white Christians, a mob destroyed his home.[15]

By the 1790s, couples like Violet and Boston King, formerly of Massachusetts, were ready to emigrate once again. In 1791, their opportunity came in the form of the Sierra Leone Company, which offered refuge to "such Free Blacks as are able to produce to their Agents, Lieutenant Clarkson, of His Majesty's Navy, and Mr. Lawrence Hartshorne, of Halifax, or either of them, satisfactory Testimonials of their Characters, (more particularly as to Honesty, Sobriety, and Industry)." In February 1792 fifteen ships carrying 1,196 blacks from Nova Scotia and New Brunswick sailed from Halifax to the colony in West Africa. Legend has it that, as they disembarked, these women and men sang, "The day of jubilee is come, return ye ransomed sinners home."[16]

And what of the African Americans who remained in the new United States? When the Revolution began, a small number of whites and blacks had voiced their hopes that the principles of liberty and freedom would bring an end to the institution of slavery. One of the most impressive voices was that of a young slave woman named Phillis Wheatley. Phillis was brought to America in 1761 at the age of seven, and sold to a prosperous Boston tailor named John Wheatley. John and his wife recognized and nurtured the talents of this young girl, allowing her to study Latin and Greek as well as to master English. Before the decade was over Phillis had created a sensation in Massachusetts with the publication of a poem honoring the evangelical preacher George Whitefield. In 1776, she published a collection of her poetry, which asserted that Africans, like Europeans, were children of God and thus deserved respect and sympathy. Phillis understood the racism that pervaded much of white society: "Some view our sable race with scornful eye / 'Their colour is a diabolic die,'" she wrote. But she continued:

> *Remember*, Christians, Negroes, *black as* Cain,
> *May be refin'd, and join th'angelic train.*[17]

Phillis won her own freedom from her master, but other blacks were not so fortunate. Indeed, there were few avenues to emancipation during the war for those who supported the patriot cause. Service in the military, for example, did not guarantee black men their freedom. The Massachusetts state government did buy and emancipate slaves who were willing to serve in the military, but other states did not follow suit. Instead, slave owners in every region began a practice of sending able-bodied slaves as their substitutes when they were drafted. In several southern states, governments chose to offer a healthy black male slave as a bonus to any white recruit who signed up for the duration of the war.[18]

The American army did not issue proclamations offering freedom to slaves who deserted their loyalist masters, nor was it American policy to encourage runaways. When loyalist plantations were captured, slave women and children were frequently taken and sold for the soldiers' profit. Slave women could be found in American army camps, where they were set to work building roads, constructing fortifications, and laundering uniforms, but they remained slaves rather than refugees. Masters usually hired these women out to the military, sometimes hiring out their children as well.

Slowly, the new northern states did take steps to eliminate slavery. Vermont's state constitution, drafted in 1777, specifically prohibited the institution. Three years later, in 1780, the Pennsylvania legislature enacted a gradual emancipation law that directly connected the ideals of the Revolution with the rights of African Americans to freedom. In its preamble, these legislators declared that "we conceive that it is our duty, and we rejoice that it is in our power, to extend a portion of that freedom to others, which hath been extended to us, and release them from the state of thralldom, to which we ourselves were tyrannically doomed, and from which we have now every prospect of being delivered." And, in a statement that echoed, unintentionally no doubt, Phillis Wheatley's insistence on universal humanity, they added: "It is not for us to inquire why, in the creation of mankind, the inhabitants of the several parts of the earth were distinguished by a difference in feature or complexion. It is sufficient to know that all are the work of the Almighty

Hand." And, in Massachusetts, a judge ruled that slavery was unconstitutional because it was in conflict with the state's bill of rights, which declared "all men . . . free and equal."[19]

The Massachusetts decision was the result of a lawsuit by a middle-aged slave woman known as Mumbet. Mumbet belonged to a prominent and respected Massachusetts lawyer and member of the state legislature, Colonel John Ashley. In 1781, Mumbet sued for her freedom in the Berkshire County Court of Common Pleas at Great Barrington, Massachusetts. Theodore Sedgwick, a rising young lawyer and political leader who would later become an abolitionist, agreed to take Mumbet's case. He successfully argued that slavery was incompatible with the guarantee of liberty in the 1780 state constitution. After the court ruled in her favor, Mumbet took the name Elizabeth Freeman. When asked what motivated her to demand her freedom, Mumbet is alleged to have said she learned about liberty by "keepin' still and mindin' things."[20]

In the southern states, however, the legacy of the Revolution was a hardening of attitudes toward emancipation and harsher laws regulating African American life. The war had taken a brutal toll in this region; by the time peace came, the plantation-based economy of the Chesapeake was badly damaged and the economy of the Lower South was in ruins. White southerners, returning home from military service, recorded their shock at the devastation and destruction. In South Carolina, the labor force had all but vanished. In the months before the British evacuated Savannah, fewer than eighty slaves were for sale in the entire state of Georgia. The destruction of property and fields and the disappearance of a labor force meant agricultural production for the market was impossible in the years immediately following Yorktown. Any slaves remaining on the plantations had to be set to work producing basic necessities such as cloth or repairing roads and houses. Thus, after the Revolution it was not an end to slavery that rice planters wanted; it was a massive infusion of new slaves from Africa or the Caribbean.[21]

The presence of black leaders, whose wartime experiences equipped them to organize resistance to slavery, acted to deepen white hostility to and fear of African Americans in these southern states. In the decade after the Revolution, assaults on whites increased across the South. More than 148 blacks were convicted of murdering whites between 1785 and 1794 in Virginia alone. From the swamps along the Savannah River, runaway slaves, both women and men, launched guerrilla attacks on plantations. In response, the new state governments tightened regulations on African Americans, forbidding slave literacy and enforcing rigid segregation laws. Individual planters inflicted brutal reprisals against slaves suspected of plotting rebellions. A racial ideology that declared African Americans inherently and irrevocably inferior took hold. This ideology could be seen during the debate over the Virginia Declaration of Rights. When some members voiced concerns that the first article, stating that "all men are by nature equally free," might spur slaves to demand their rights, supporters of the article dismissed these concerns. They assured their fellow political leaders that "slaves not being constituent members of our society could never pretend to any benefit from such a maxim."[22]

In the end, there would be no winning side for Hannah or Mary Postill, or for the many nameless African American women who died of starvation and enemy attack. Many African American women who won their freedom lost it again through violence and trickery and the venality of men entrusted with their care. Many more died in the attempt to gain it. Those who succeeded faced racial prejudice in exile that resulted in poverty and injustice. Those who remained behind in the South found the reins of slavery tighten around them. The American Revolution had brought no "day of jubilee" after all.

CHAPTER 9

"IT WAS I WHO DID IT"

*Spies, Saboteurs, Couriers,
and Other Heroines*

Like all wars, the American Revolution created opportunities for heroism by ordinary people. Farmers and shopkeepers, schoolteachers and servants—men whose daily life did not hint at the resourcefulness and bravery they discovered within themselves during the long home-front war. Much of this heroism was manifested on the battlefield, but this was not its only venue. Men like Paul Revere and Nathan Hale risked their lives and property as spies, couriers, and saboteurs, earning their place in our historical memory for acts of bravery and sacrifice for their chosen cause. What is less well known is that women and girls earned a place in the pantheon of heroes too.

Over the course of the war, teenage girls and middle-aged matrons left behind their household chores and ventured behind enemy lines, risked capture and arrest, and stood up to armed soldiers who entered their homes and shops. Many of their stories come down to us only through family tales, told and retold, exaggerated and embellished in the process, but with a kernel of truth nevertheless. They have appeared on websites and in essays created by proud descendants who have access to diaries, letters, or other records of their ancestors. They have also appeared in the works of genealogists and town historians who scoured local archives and took oral histories from survivors of the war. And, since the 1970s, they have reappeared in the works of amateur historians whose imaginations have been captured by them. Finally, many have made their way into scholarly books and articles, where the many versions have been analyzed and evaluated. In every case, these stories survive because that kernel of truth found within them captures a wartime reality out of which myths are made.[1]

These stories of Revolutionary War heroines reveal surprising humor and resourcefulness. In them, young girls chew and swallow documents rather than have them discovered by the enemy; middle-aged women listen at keyholes to spy on military planning sessions; and old women serve liquor to soldiers and rob them of their guns. To achieve their ends, these women often played on the gender expectations and stereotypes of their day, feigning innocence or employing charms and wiles to gain the trust of the enemy. At other times, they demonstrated the steely determination of mothers seeking to protect their families, of sisters devoted to brothers in uniform, and of wives who admired the political choices their husbands had made and embraced the political cause their husbands served. But wherever the war front moved—from New England to Charleston to the middle states, and back to the South once again—women became veterans of the struggle. The tales that follow are only a small sampling of their feats.

In the same year that Paul Revere and William Dawes made their fateful ride to call the men of Lexington and Concord "to arms!" a twenty-two-year-old Connecticut woman named Deborah Champion mounted a horse and rode toward Boston. She carried with her important dispatches for General George Washington, the commander in chief of the Continental Army. By any standard, Champion was an unlikely hero. Unlike Paul Revere, she had played no role in radical politics before the Revolution; she was neither a Continental soldier nor a member of the local militia. But when a young horseman rode into her yard and rushed into the house to confer with Deborah's father, Colonel Henry Champion, her adventure began. The intelligence the exhausted rider carried had to reach General Washington—and Deborah and her father believed she was the person to carry it.

The next morning, before it was truly light, Deborah Champion, accompanied by a family servant, Aristarchus, rode due north to the Massachusetts border. The route was not the quickest, but it was the safest, for the British were already at Providence, Rhode Island. Although the roads were rutted from recent rains, the two riders made good time, passing through Norwich, then up the valley of the Quinebaug River to Canterbury. Here they rested for an hour before pushing on toward Pomfret, passing fields left in the care of old men and women by farmers gone to war. Changing horses at her uncle's farm, Deborah determined to ride on through the night, the dispatches hidden in a small compartment of her saddlebags, under the food her mother had packed for the journey.

Just as dawn was breaking, she was stopped by a sentry and ordered to dismount. His intention was to take her to his commanding officer, but Deborah, thinking quickly, warned him that it was too early to disturb the sleep of his superior. The young redcoat hesitated, uncertain what to do. He looked again at his captive, whose hair and face were shrouded by a large hood. In the dim light, she seemed to be no more than an old woman, traveling with an old servant, no doubt on her way as she claimed to visit an ailing friend nearby. No need to bother the sleeping officer. Released, Deborah and Aristarchus rode on to Boston and delivered the papers into the hands of George Washington. The general, Deborah later reported to a friend, "was pleased to compliment me most highly as to what he was pleased to call the courage I had displayed and my patriotism."[2]

Far to the south, as the British besieged the

South Carolina capital of Charleston in early 1776, Harriet Prudence Patterson Hall and three of her friends made their way past enemy soldiers surrounding the city. When the sentries stopped them, Hall explained that they were on their way to purchase medicine from a Charleston apothecary. What the redcoats saw gave them little reason to be suspicious: standing before them were four well-dressed matrons, on an errand that took them into the city. The British soldiers stepped aside, giving the women permission to pass. With that, Harriet Hall walked into Charleston, an important message for the American commander safely hidden inside her petticoat.[3]

Charleston was not the only city in peril in 1776. That year, New York fell, and it remained under British occupation for the rest of the war. Despite Washington's efforts to defend the city, the defeat of his raw recruits in the battle of Long Island and the battle of White Plains sent the Continental Army fleeing for its life across the Hudson River. Only a small number of artillery companies remained at Fort Washington, perched high above the river, at the northern tip of Manhattan. On November 16, this fort came under attack. Among those inside were John Corbin, an enlisted man, and his twenty-five-year-old wife, Margaret Cochran Corbin. When the assault began, John took his position as an assistant gunner, but soon had to take over the cannon when the gunner was killed. Margaret immediately stepped into John's place, helping her husband load the cannon until he too fell dead. Margaret had no time to grieve. She stepped again into John's place, loading and firing the cannon herself. Suddenly, she felt a searing pain as grapeshot struck her shoulder, chest, and jaw. Seeing Margaret fall, soldiers rushed to carry her away from the front line and placed her in the care of other camp followers who were tending the wounded.

When the Americans at Fort Washington surrendered, the British set the wounded soldiers free on parole. Margaret was among them. They were ferried across the river to Fort Lee, and from there Margaret was taken by wagon to Pennsylvania. In time, her jaw and chest lacerations healed, but Margaret Cochran Corbin never recovered the use of her left arm. In an unusual move, Congress acknowledged her military contribution and granted her "half the pay and allowances of a soldier in service." But if her veteran's pension sustained her, it could not ensure a happy ending to her story. After the war, Margaret moved to Highland Falls, New York. There she became a figure of scorn rather than admiration. When she died in 1800, few local citizens realized that the sharp-tongued, alcoholic woman known as "Dirty Kate" had taken "a soldier's part in the war for liberty."[4]

On a dark night in April 1777, a sixteen-year-old rider named Sybil Ludington sped along the rough roads of Putnam County, New York, stopping at farmhouse doors only long enough to rouse the men sleeping inside. Her father, Colonel Henry Ludington, had received word that his New York militia was needed in the defense of Danbury, Connecticut, and Sybil's mission was to deliver the call to arms. Because of her, the Putnam militia played a critical role in the Danbury battle. Although Governor William Tryon and his redcoats managed to destroy the arms depot at Danbury, the Ludington troops helped Generals Benedict Arnold and David Wooster drive the British from the town.[5]

By the fall of 1777, Philadelphia was in the hands of the British, and by December, Sir William Howe and his officers were enjoying a winter round of balls and banquets while General Washington and his men were temporarily encamped at nearby Whitemarsh. Howe had taken up residence on Second Street, in the elegant home of John Cadwalader, a neighbor of a quiet and unassuming Quaker couple, William and Lydia Darragh. Soon after Howe moved in, a young British major knocked on the Darraghs' door and demanded that their house, too, be turned over to British officers. Lydia Darragh pleaded with the officer to reconsider: she had two small children and the family had nowhere to go. A compromise was struck: the Darraghs could remain, but a room in their home was to be kept at the ready, in case Howe needed it for a military staff meeting.

On December 2, the British collected on Lydia's

promise. An officer arrived, instructed Lydia to prepare candles for the meeting room, and then ordered the Darragh family to retire early. The officer would knock on Lydia's bedroom door, he explained, when the general and his staff had departed. It was obvious that something important was on the agenda—and, overcome with a "presentment of evil," Lydia decided to find out what it was. This was no idle curiosity on her part; as a supporter of the American cause, Lydia had already sent military intelligence to Washington's camp, using her fourteen-year-old son, John, as a courier to her oldest son, who was a lieutenant in the Continental Army. And so, despite the risk involved, she laid her plans for the evening. When the British had assembled, Lydia slipped silently down the stairs to the meeting room door and put her ear to the keyhole. Listening intently, she was able to overhear Howe and his officers. What she heard confirmed her worst fears: the British were planning an attack against Washington's camp on December 4.

As the meeting broke up, Lydia returned to her bed. Anxious not to arouse any suspicions, she pretended to be so deeply asleep that it took several sharp raps on her bedroom door to awaken her. Looking drowsy, she at last opened the door and said her goodnights to the British officer. Then Lydia lay down to think. It was one thing to know what Howe planned; it was another to figure out how to get that information to the Americans. The

British did not allow free access in and out of the city, and anyone asking for a permit to travel to the countryside needed a good excuse. But before the night was over, Lydia believed she had come up with just the right ruse.

The following day, Lydia Darragh went to Howe's headquarters and requested a pass to go to the village of Frankford to purchase flour. The officer in charge saw a middle-aged matron, carrying an empty flour sack, anxious to provide bread for her family's table. What he did not see was a clever spy with top secret information hidden away within the folds of her dress. Permit in hand, Lydia set out on foot through the snow, to deliver the news of the impending attack. When the British made their move on the Continental troops at Whitemarsh the following day, they found Washington and his men ready, armed, and waiting. That evening, Lydia Darragh had the satisfaction of knowing that the surprise attack had been no surprise at all.[6]

Not every daring woman was a daughter of liberty, of course. Some, like Ann Bates, were loyal supporters of the Crown. Before the war, Ann was a Philadelphia schoolteacher, but by 1778, she was one of General Henry Clinton's most effective spies. When the British evacuated Philadelphia in July 1778, Ann went with them, following her new husband, who was a soldier in His Majesty's army. Once she arrived in British-occupied New York, she was approached and asked to serve as a spy.

Under the cover name of "Mrs. Barnes" Ann slipped into the Continental Army encampment at White Plains, New York, posing as one of the many female peddlers who populated every military camp. In this guise, she moved freely about the camp, for American officers, like their British counterparts, assumed that women knew too little about military equipment or military strategy to make effective intelligence reports. It was a reasonable assumption—in most cases. But not when it came to "Mrs. Barnes." This schoolteacher had an advantage few women enjoyed: a husband who repaired cannon, guns, and other weapons for the army. Ann's reports on cannons, men, and munitions were as thorough as most men's would be.

In addition to being more knowledgeable than a woman was assumed to be, Ann Bates was fearless. On one of her missions, when an inside contact in the American army failed to materialize, Ann refused to abandon her assignment. She managed to penetrate into the inner sanctum of Washington's headquarters, where, as she put it, "I had the Opportunity of going through their whole Army Remarking at the same time the strength & Situation of each Brigade, & the Number of Cannon with their Situation and Weight of Ball each Cannon was Charged with." In August 1778, Ann's intelligence about troop movements spurred General Clinton to send reinforcements to Rhode Island. The Americans and the French paid a heavy price for their assumption that a woman peddler was no security risk: they were forced to retreat from Newport and Rhode Island remained in British hands.[7]

Many miles away, in early 1779, "the biggest, the tallest, the most imposing Negress" in the state of Georgia, known only as Mammy Kate, mounted a horse named Lightfoot and rode fifty miles to the British fort at Augusta. There, her master, Stephen Heard, was one of twenty-three patriots who had been captured by loyalist forces and imprisoned at Fort Cornwallis. Mammy Kate was determined to rescue Heard from certain execution. Leaving Lightfoot safely hidden outside of town, she acquired a large clothes basket and made her way on foot to the fort. She offered her services to the redcoats as a washerwoman, and soon had a thriving clientele of British officers who admired her skillful ironing of their ruffled shirts. Having ingratiated herself with the officers, she took the next step in her rescue plan: asking permission to do the prisoner Heard's laundry as well. Heard's jailers agreed. Twice a week for the next several weeks, Mammy Kate entered Heard's prison cell, delivering freshly laundered linens and leaving with a load of dirty ones in the basket on her head. One evening, as dusk was falling, Mammy Kate entered the prison cell and exited with her basket, balanced on her head as usual. But no dirty laundry filled the basket that evening: curled up inside was the diminutive Stephen Heard.

Once outside the city, Mammy Kate set her basket down, and she and Heard made their way quickly to where Lightfoot and a second horse, stolen by Kate from under the noses of the British stable guards, now waited. Heard, who went on to be governor of the state of Georgia, freed his rescuer and gave her a small tract of land and a new home. Although a free woman, Kate continued to work for the Heard family until her death.[8]

In 1780, the war was going badly for southern patriots. Charleston had fallen to the enemy in May and the defeated American officers and soldiers inside the city had been taken prisoner. Loyalists and redcoats freely roamed the country-side, taking towns and strategic posts, almost at will. The rebellion, British commander Henry Clinton boasted, was over in South Carolina. But many of those who refused to renew oaths of allegiance to the king fled to North Carolina and from there began to harass the British troops whenever possible. The enemy responded with raids on patriot sympathizers, especially those suspected of hiding caches of ammunition or weapons for the guerrilla bands. In the spring of 1780, the back-country home of Jane Black Thomas became one of their targets. Jane's husband, Colonel John Thomas, was miles away, fighting near Charleston, and only a small band of patriot soldiers had been assigned to protect the Thomas family and the much-needed military supplies buried in the yard. As 150 loyalists approached the Thomas property, the patriot soldiers gathered all the ammunition they could and rode off to hide it once again. This left Jane, her three daughters, her young son, and her son-in-law Josiah Culbertson to detain the loyalists long enough for the patriots to make good their escape. Josiah set up rifle slots all around the house; Jane and her children formed a bullet brigade, feeding bullets to Josiah at each rifle station. The ruse worked for a while, for the loyalists believed the house was filled with soldiers. But when the enemy finally decided to charge the house, Jane sprang into action. Brandishing a sword in her hands, she stood in front of her home, daring her attackers to enter. Stunned, and apparently intimidated by the threat of violence from a middle-aged matron, the loyalists withdrew. The ammunition saved by her exploits was later used by General Thomas Sumter at the battle of Hanging Rock.[9]

Jane Thomas's home was not the only hiding place for the South Carolina patriots' vital supply of ammunition in 1780. Other caches could be found in hollow trees or dry wells, and necessity often required that women be charged with their safekeeping. One of these women was Martha Bratton, whose husband was a leader of the guerrilla resistance. Martha was warned that a detachment of loyalists was on the way to seize the supplies in her care. Knowing that she could not defend the cache, she decided on the next best thing: she would destroy it. Acting quickly, she laid down a train of powder from the cache to the spot near her home where she stood. As the loyalists rode into sight, she set fire to the powder train— and stood calmly through the explosion. When the infuriated commanding officer demanded to know where the man was who had destroyed his prize, Martha Bratton was said to have calmly replied: "It was I who did it."[10]

Other southern women proved willing to destroy their own homes rather than allow a loyalist or British victory. In 1781, British troops had seized the home of Rebecca Brewton Motte and turned it into a fortification, adding a stockade and a ditch around it. That May, a patriot force laid siege to "Fort Motte," hoping to drive the enemy from the area. When news came that the British were sending reinforcements from Camden, South Carolina, the Americans decided their only hope was to shoot flaming arrows at the roof of the Motte home, setting fire to it and forcing the soldiers inside to evacuate. Reluctantly, they explained their plan to Rebecca Motte, who had taken up residence in a house nearby. Motte did not hesitate; not only did she give them permission to destroy her home, she handed the officers a beautifully crafted bow and a bundle of arrows— and watched while her house went up in flames.[11]

In the summer of 1781, the patriot prospects in the South remained dim. Yorktown was still in the future, and, for the moment, the army of General Nathanael Greene was in retreat before the British troops under Lord Rawdon. Hoping to turn the hunter into the hunted, Greene decided to send a message to General Thomas Sumter to join him in an attack on Rawdon's army. But the countryside was filled with loyalists and no one could be found to carry the word from one general to the other. No man could be found, that is. But a young girl named Emily Geiger came forward to volunteer. Somewhat reluctantly, Greene agreed. He not only entrusted a letter to Sumter to her safekeeping but also gave her the message verbally, in case she needed to destroy the written evidence.

Riding sidesaddle, Emily Geiger set off on the pretense of visiting her uncle several miles away. She stopped that evening at a farmhouse, where she was given supper and a room. Before she retired, she realized that her hosts were loyalists. In the middle of the night, she heard a rider dismount and ask if the farmer had seen a young girl pass by. As Emily feared, the farmer revealed her presence. Confident that he could get a good night's sleep before taking Emily prisoner, the loyalist soldier settled in for the night. Emily saw her chance: she slipped out an open window, saddled her horse, and rode on through the night. Her luck ran out the next evening, however, when she was intercepted by a British scouting party. Since she was coming from the direction of Greene's camp, the soldiers decided to detain her. Although they were eager to examine her for hidden documents, the men balked at performing the search of a young lady themselves. Instead they sent for a loyalist matron. Emily took advantage of the delay: she tore Greene's letter into small pieces and ate them, one by one. The search revealed nothing. The scouts' commanding officer apologized and, to make amends, provided Emily with an escort to her uncle's home. From there, Emily made her way to Sumter's camp, delivered the message verbally, and had the satisfaction of seeing Sumter's men immediately head north to join General Greene at Orangeburgh.[12]

In October 1781, Lord Cornwallis surrendered to General George Washington at Yorktown. Fighting continued, however, for over a year, especially along the Pennsylvania border. Here, on September 12, 1782, some 250 Indians and 40 British soldiers laid siege to a small frontier outpost named Fort Henry. Inside the men and boys defending the fort ran dangerously low on ammunition. Their supplies were tantalizingly close, in a cabin about sixty yards from the southeastern corner of the fort, but anyone who dared cross the open space between the cabin and the fort would be an easy target for the besiegers. To the amazement of British and Indian soldiers alike, the gates of the fort swung open around noontime, and a young girl ran toward the cabin. A few moments later, she re-emerged, carrying a large bundle wrapped in her apron. When they realized that gunpowder was inside that bundle, the Indians opened fire. With lightning speed, the girl reached the gate—and disappeared from view. The girl was Betsy Zane, and her daring allowed the Americans to hold off their attackers. The British and the Indians abandoned their attempt to seize Fort Henry the following day.[13]

The young girls and matrons, the schoolteachers and African American slaves, the wealthy widows and camp followers whose stories are preserved in local histories and family scrapbooks rather than scholarly tomes give evidence that life during the American Revolution was indeed, as the popular British song put it, "the world turned upside down." The war for independence allowed, and often propelled, these women to step out of their traditional female roles for the briefest of moments and to perform deeds that surprised them perhaps as much as they surprised others. When the war ended, however, these women returned to their kitchens and parlors, to nurseries and gardens— and to the anonymity their society considered appropriately feminine. The lives of the women whose stories are told in this chapter were comfortably unremarkable after the war. Lydia Darragh returned to the life of a Quaker matron. Emily Geiger married a planter and raised a family. Mammy Kate had nine children and was buried in an unmarked grave near Stephen Heard and his wife. Rebecca Motte never remarried, but she rebuilt the home she had helped destroy. Martha Bratton lived for many years after peace returned, a "notable housewife" on her husband's farm. Ann Bates sailed to England with her husband in 1781. When he later deserted her, she was given a small pension for her work as a British spy. No reports on Deborah Champion, Sybil Ludington, or Betsy Zane can be found. In their return to ordinary lives and familiar gender roles, these women share a bond with the thousands of American soldiers who became, once again, farmers and farm laborers, planters and merchants, dock workers and shopkeepers when the war was over.

CHAPTER 10

"THERE IS NO SEX IN SOUL"

The Legacy of Revolution

After World War I, Warren G. Harding captured the nation's mood with his campaign slogan promising a "return to normalcy." Harding's vocabulary was flawed, but his perception of the public's wishes was accurate. Across the centuries, Americans in 1783 would have understood this intense desire to pick up the pieces of a prewar life. Their long struggle for independence had produced a daring experiment in government, creating a republic that altered many white men's relationship to the state, redefined the source of sovereignty, and introduced a new nation among nations. Now the radical impulse behind these innovations seemed spent.

For eight years, American women and men had been caught up in extraordinary drama and crisis, surrounded by violence and death. If they had discovered within themselves untapped reserves of courage and resiliency, by 1783 they nevertheless longed for the comforting demands of ordinary life. Reconstructing that life would not prove easy, for the world many Americans remembered, and hoped to return to, was a shambles. In the South, what one planter called "this cursed war" had left plantations and farms in ruins; in New York and New Jersey, cities and countryside bore the scars of long periods of enemy occupation; in New England, peace had brought economic depression, farm foreclosures, and unemployment in its wake. A new struggle to restore "normalcy," or to re-create an acceptable version of it, would occupy the energies and attention of Americans for years to come.[1]

For the lucky few, the return to normalcy meant a liberation from sacrifice and somber reflection. By 1783, the wealthy Philadelphian Nancy Shippen had marked war's end by abandoning patriotic homespun for "an elegant French hat with five white plumes nodding in different ways." And in Virginia, where young Betsy Ambler had once recorded her frantic flight from the British army, sixteen-year-old Lucinda Lee, daughter of an elite planter, now filled her diary with accounts of postwar parties, dances, flirtations, and the clothes imported from London by her friends. And at Harvard College, John Quincy Adams recorded the return of traditional student antics—getting drunk and smashing windows—by the sons of wealthy merchants, ministers, and political leaders.[2]

Yet for a small group of elite American women and men—poets, essayists, educators, and political leaders—it seemed essential to pause and to consider the lessons the Revolution offered, if any, for women and to decide what changes in women's roles might prove necessary in the new republican society. For a brief but intense postwar moment, these intellectuals engaged in a lively debate over what in the next century came to be called "the woman question." In their arguments, these women and men wove together prewar trends and postwar possibilities. Although they spoke of the Revolution as a watershed, a transforming event, their ideas suggest instead that the Revolution was a hothouse, forcing into bloom gender roles and gender ideals that had been planted long before the Stamp Act and the Boston Tea Party set the colonies on the path to independence. To the twenty-first-century reader, some of what they say will sound modern; they were, after all, the children of the Enlightenment, members of the generation on this side of the Atlantic who ushered in a secular, scientific view of the world and endorsed a belief in the rationality of human beings, the efficacy of education, and the ability of parents and teachers to shape the character of children through instruction and example. Their spirit will strike a familiar chord in the modern sensibility as well. In the nineteenth century, despite the rise of Romanticism and sentimentality, the antebellum and Progressive Era reformers who believed in the perfectibility of society are their heirs. And in the twentieth century, despite the pessimism of postmodernism, their implicit faith in progress remains strong. Yet much of what they understood to be a radical departure would be labeled social conservatism today. Like reformers of any age, their vision of the future was created in the context of their present and in reaction to their past.

The women and men who filled pages of essays, novels, speeches, and poems with thoughts on the woman question were members of an intellectual vanguard. Some, like Susanna Haskell Rowson, novelist, poet, playwright, actress, and educator, were part of a transatlantic cultural community that had linked Americans with the broader world of British and continental European intellectual and creative life before the Revolution. Others, like the essayist Judith Sargent Murray, came out of the liberal religious movement of prewar New England. Still others—like Benjamin Rush, physician, political leader, and educator, who, before the war, had traveled to Scotland for his medical education—reflected the growth of the scientific community in the colonies. If they were far more cosmopolitan than their neighbors, they were also far more economically privileged. Their privileged social status shaped their perceptions of the problems the new nation faced as well as the lessons the Revolution had taught just as it shaped their agendas for women in the new nation. The typical woman they conjured up when they spoke of the American woman was not Margaret Corbin or Mammy Kate, but a wo-man of their own race and social class. And the issues they considered important to that woman were not necessarily the issues facing frontier girls like Betsy Zane or newly freed domestic servants like Mumbet. Like these ordinary women, Abigail Adams and Judith Sargent Murray saw the world through the lens of their own social realities. Nevertheless, many of their arguments about woman's nature and certainly many of the changes they proposed in women's social roles would have altered the circumstances in which all American women lived.[3]

The postwar debate on the woman question began with a resounding rejection of the traditional notion that women were both morally and mentally inferior to men. The Quaker poet Susanna Wright, for example, challenged the religious basis for man's intellectual and moral superiority. "Reason rules, in every one, the same," she wrote. "No Right, has Man, his Equal to controul, / Since, all agree, There is no Sex in soul."[4] In a letter to a friend in 1777, Judith Sargent Murray took the argument further, standing the lesson to be garnered from the tale of Original Sin on its head:

That Eve was indeed the weaker vessel, I boldly take upon me to deny—Nay, it should seem she was abundantly the stronger vessel since all the deep laid Art of the most subtle fiend that inhabited the infernal regions, was requisite to draw her from her allegiance, while Adam was overcome by the influence of the softer passions merely by his attachment to a female . . .[5]

The mental and moral inferiority of women had been attacked before the Revolution, of course. But the war did more than provide additional fodder for philosophical arguments over gender. Women's participation in the war had given concrete, empirical evidence of their ability to think rationally and make ethical judgments. Since the first protests against British taxation policies, they had formed political commitments and demonstrated their patriotism. There could be little debate that women like Esther deBerdt Reed, who spearheaded the fund-raising drive in Philadelphia, and Mercy Otis Warren, playwright and propagandist in pre-Revolutionary Boston, like their husbands, had understood the choice confronting them between continued loyalty to the Crown or independence. The experience of the Revolution thus confirmed the Enlightenment theories that preceded it.

Writers like Wright and Murray also challenged secular assumptions of women's inferiority that grew out of the rise of a prosperous class in the colonies. In eighteenth-century America, as in England, satires and sermons had condemned women for the vanity, superficiality, and materialism that seemed to mark the darker side of gentility. Wright, Murray, and other women intellectuals argued that these defects were not the fault of women's natural weaknesses or limited capacities; instead, the problem could be traced to the poor education their sex had received. The vanity and frivolous behavior critics observed in women were clearly the fruits of social injustice: women had been denied access to formal knowledge at the same time that they were actively encouraged to value beauty over intelligence. In a world where a wag could declare, "Girls knew quite enough if they could make a shirt and a pudding," what chance did women have to demonstrate their more serious aspirations? The blame for women's folly must be laid at society's doorstep.[6]

This analysis led Murray, Susanna Rowson, and Dr. Rush to the same conclusion: formal education was essential to cultivate women's dormant rationality and morality. As reformers, they campaigned for the creation of schools for women that would offer challenging and rigorous curricula rather than lessons in refinement. Geography, not dancing; political philosophy rather than fine needlework—these courses would not only awaken women's intellect but ensure their rejection of luxury and vanity. These claims did not go uncontested. Critics warned that formal education would create masculine women, unattractive in their appearance, negligent in their duties to husbands and family. A knowledge of geography, political theory, and history would inevitably result in a monster, "disgustingly slovenly in her person" and "indecent in her habits."[7]

Despite strong opposition from these critics, the campaign for female education was remarkably successful. In 1787, the doors of the Philadelphia Young Ladies Academy opened, ushering in a revolution in education in the new nation. Similar academies and boarding schools sprang up in New England, the middle states, and the South. The course of study in most cases was the same as the course of study offered in boys' preparatory academies and included history, rhetoric, geography, English composition, and mathematics. This revolution in education was so successful that, by the end of the eighteenth century, elite society frowned upon a poorly educated young woman.[8]

What accounted for this success? Why, that is, was it now so important to free women from the foibles associated with their sex? The answer lay in the concept of a republic and in the formula that political leaders believed held the key to the survival of that republic. Unlike monarchies, they argued, republics depended upon the rectitude and the patriotism of their collective sovereign: the citizens. Republics required a constant renewal of devotion and self-sacrifice in order to survive. They required informed citizens, able to resist the siren call of the tyrant and the temptations of corruption. Thus, patriotism had to be instilled in each succeeding generation if representative government was to endure. To whom should this vital task of raising patriots be entrusted?

Those who raised this question turned to the family for its answer. In colonial America, fathers had been responsible for the moral education of their sons and daughters. But the contours of the new nation's economy were shifting: the business of prosperous men of commerce, agriculture, and law was moving out of the household. At the same time, the household production that marked the busy day of the notable housewife was contracting. Even before the Revolution, prosperous women, aided by markets in the cities and by slave labor in the South, had seen the duties of housewifery diminish. Indeed, before the decade of protest and the Revolution, increased leisure time seemed to be an identifying mark of the wealthy matron and her daughters. What women did with their leisure time before the Revolution—whether they used it to read novels, decorate their homes, socialize with their peers, or instruct their children— seemed to be a personal, private choice. But during the Revolution, women's choices became politicized. Every woman who raised money for the troops or nursed the sick and wounded rather than retiring to her parlor to read a book or paying a visit to a friend was declaring that her leisure time had civic value.

Thus, after the war, the intellectual recognition of women as rational beings combined with the economic reality of a decline in household production to produce a shift in prosperous women's familial role. It was a matter of emphasis and priorities rather than a newly carved out role, but it transformed the notable housewife into the republican wife and mother. It was the republican mother who would inscribe patriotism upon what Enlightenment philosophers called the blank slate, or "tabula rasa," of childhood. And it was the republican wife who would keep her husband virtuous by her example. As one postwar young woman put it, her task was to "inspire her brothers, her husband, and her sons, with such a love of virtue, such just ideas of the true value of civil liberty . . . that future heroes and statesmen . . . shall exhaltingly declare, it is to my mother I owe this elevation."[9]

It stood to reason that if mothers were to be responsible for rearing patriotic sons and daughters, then society must arm them with the knowledge necessary to the task. Mothers must know enough about government and politics, about past republican experiments and the causes of their failure, about science and its empirical mode of thinking, and about moral philosophy to socialize their children for citizenship in the new nation. Thus the knowledge of history, political theory, and moral philosophy acquired in the young ladies' academies was not to be an end in itself, an experience of personal growth and self-exploration. It was to have practical value and social significance: republican mothers would nurture republican children. Benjamin Rush provided this rationale in his *Thoughts upon Female Education, Accommodated to the Present State of Society, Manners, and Government in the United*

States of America. "The equal share that every citizen has in the liberty and the possible share he may have in the government of our country," he wrote, "makes it necessary that our ladies should be qualified to a certain degree, by a peculiar and suitable education, to concur in instructing their sons in the principles of liberty and government."[10]

Radical though Rush's vision was, it did not break free of the demands of gentility. The good doctor did not advocate a total abandonment of lessons in dancing, singing, and needlework. But in providing the raison d'être for their inclusion in the curriculum, he confirmed a shift in the meaning of "helpmate" that had begun when the eighteenth century was young. "Vocal music," he wrote in his *Thoughts upon Female Education,* "should never be neglected in the education of a young lady . . . it will enable her to soothe the care of domestic life. The distress and vexation of a husband, the noise of the nursery, and even the sorrows that will sometimes intrude into her own bosom may all be relieved by a song. . . ." A well-educated wife, Rush was arguing, would develop the genteel arts in order to bring solace to her husband just as she would expand her intellectual horizons in order to nurture her sons.[11]

Thus, as postwar intellectuals urged their countrymen and women to acknowledge women's moral and intellectual capacities, they drew a tight circle around the space in which she would apply them: the home and family. Yet this emerging gender ideology was not a male conspiracy. Not even the boldest of the women who engaged the woman question could envision female intellect cut free from the tethers of the helpmate role. Like their male counterparts, these women agreed that female education must be useful to someone—and that someone could not be simply the female herself. "Teach us to prize the power of intellect," Rowson had urged her male reader, and you will reap "the sweet reward" of "an affectionate and faithful wife." By the antebellum era of the nineteenth century, the glorification of the home as a "haven in a heartless world," and of that haven as a woman's domain, would carry Rush and Rowson's advice to its logical conclusion.[12]

The intellectuals who debated the woman question narrowed rather than expanded women's sphere. In stressing the importance to the republic of a mother's role in socializing the next patriotic generation, they made motherhood a civic imperative, too important to be rejected by any woman. In stressing the growing trend toward companionate marriage between husband and wife, rather than the earlier practical combination of his economic productivity in the field and hers in the household, they focused women's emotional and intellectual energies on the small circle of domesticity. If, in the process, they had increased the self-esteem of women and given their activities civic importance, they had also closed out important areas for debate. Neither expanding women's economic opportunities nor extending their legal rights found a place on the woman question agenda.

The opportunity might have arisen to discuss both. For the bleakest lesson of the Revolution was, after all, that the unexpected was very likely to happen again. The generation of Revolutionary War women had proved their mettle; they had shown themselves and their fathers, husbands, and sons that they could "make do," take over the management of farms and business, defend home and children from danger, and cope with physical dislocation and devastating reversals of fortune. But would the next generation of women be prepared if similar challenges arose? Early in the discussions, Judith Sargent Murray proposed that the republic's daughters be trained in "habits of industry and order" that would allow them "to procure for themselves the necessaries of life." Here was a radical notion: a generation of women, able to support themselves in the marketplace. Yet few of Murray's peers endorsed this practical plan for creating an independent, self-sufficient woman. Instead, they were satisfied to mold a feminine character that could endure, rather than defeat, adversity. Patience, endurance, frugality, fortitude—these were the virtues that would sustain women should the unexpected happen again.[13]

Women's economic independence and married women's legal rights remained as abysmally restricted as they had been before the war. There was no public demand to reform the legal status of *feme covert* that left married women without the right to own or buy land, to sue or be sued, or to claim as her property the clothes on her back. No one took up the suggestion made by Abigail Adams in 1776, even before independence was declared, that political leaders "Remember the Ladies" as they made new laws for a new nation. Adams had been quick to see the irony in her husband's demand for an end to tyranny and the limits of his zeal for independence. "I long to hear that you have declared an independency," she began in her letter to John of March 31, 1776,

> and by the way in the new Code of Laws which I suppose it will be necessary for you to make I desire that you would Remember the Ladies, and be more generous and favourable to them than your ancestors. Do not put such unlimited power into the hands of the Husbands. Remember all Men would be tyrants if they could.

Abigail was not asking her husband for woman suffrage. She was asking for a revision of those laws that deprived a married woman of most of her legal identity, placing her in the same dependent category as children and the insane. John understood his wife's meaning all too well. Ready to rebel against the unlimited power of king and Parliament, John Adams was not ready to see the hierarchy of gender destroyed in the process. "As to your extraordinary Code of Laws," he replied on April 14, 1776, "I cannot but laugh." His patronizing tone immediately gave way, however, to a nightmare vision of *his* world turned upside down: "We have been told that our Struggle has loosened the bands of Government everywhere. That Children and Apprentices were disobedient—that schools and Colledges were grown turbulent—that Indians slighted their Guardians and Negroes grew insolent to their Masters. But your Letter was the first Intimation that another Tribe more numerous and powerfull than all the rest were grown discontented. . . ." That discontent could not be accommodated: "Depend upon it, We know better than to repeal our Masculine systems." Just as King George might argue that England had been a mother country, ever solicitous and protective of her colonial children, John Adams insisted to his wife that his "Masculine system" was benign rather than oppressive. "We dare not exert our Power in its full Latitude," he wrote. "We are obliged to go fair, and softly, and in Practice We are the subjects. We have only the Name of Masters, and rather than give up this, which would completely subject Us to the Despotism of the Peticoat, I hope General Washington and all our brave Heroes would fight." In Adams's claim that mastery was a burden rather than a privilege, we can see an eerie echo of the

223

antebellum slave owner's claim of the burdens of his patriarchy.

Abigail attempted to have the last word in this exchange. On May 7, she again took up her pen to press John to see his masculine system for the absolutism that it was. "I can not say that I think you very generous to the Ladies, for whilst you are proclaiming peace and good will to Men, Emancipating all Nations, you insist upon retaining an absolute power over Wives." Although Abigail ended with a threat of female rebellion, she couched it in the only terms she could imagine: the Ladies would charm their masters into surrendering their power.[14]

There was no room in John Adams's masculine system for female legal or economic independence. Nor was there any room in his new republic for female political participation. While all those who debated the woman question agreed on the intellectual and moral equality of the sexes, few believed that the two sexes should employ their abilities in the same arenas. Alone among them, Judith Sargent Murray raised the possibility of women's entrance onto the political stage. In her "Observations on Female Abilities," Murray insisted that women were "as capable of supporting with honour the toils of government" as men. If a willingness and ability to lay down one's life for one's country was the sine qua non of citizenship, history—both distant and recent—provided numerous examples of women who risked their lives on the battlefield and performed those acts of heroism normally associated with men. Much like Esther deBerdt Reed's *Sentiments of an American Woman,* Murray's *Gleaner* essays reminded the reader of heroic queens and female warriors, women who ruled wisely and led their armies into battle courageously. If America had not yet produced a female Washington, this did not deny the possibility that one would arise in the future. And yet Murray, like Abigail Adams, was ultimately more comfortable calling upon women's ability to influence and persuade than upon their powers to legislate or command. If she urged women to have political interests, it was because their roles as "wives, as Mothers, and as friends" required that they care about the future of the nation.[15]

America's political leaders concurred. Influence and example were women's political tools; the ballot and the legislative halls remained men's domain. In the single state that granted women the right to vote, oversight rather than foresight was responsible. In their eagerness to prevent propertyless men from voting, New Jersey legislators drafted a constitution that defined voters only as "all free inhabitants" who met certain property and residency requirements. Thus from 1776 to 1807, New Jersey women of wealth claimed their right to vote in local elections. But in 1797, when women voters in Elizabeth, New Jersey, almost cost an ambitious candidate his election, woman suffrage became a political topic. His opponents, members of the Federalist Party, praised the women in speech and poetry, declaring

> *Let Democrats with senseless prate,*
> *Maintain the softer Sex, sir,*
> *Should ne'er with politics of State*
> *Their gentle minds perplex Sir;*
> *Such vulgar prejudice we scorn;*
> *Their sex is no objection . . .*

To many, however, their sex was indeed an objection. In October 1802, the *Trenton True American* published an article from "A Friend to the Ladies." Women's votes, the anonymous author declared, undermine representative government for they "are rarely, if ever unbiased." By nature, he continued, women were "timid and pliant, unskilled in politics, unacquainted with all the real merits of the several candidates, and almost always placed under the dependence or care of a father, uncle or brother." The result was inevitable: "they will of course be directed or persuaded by [their male protectors], and the man who brings his two daughters, his mother, his aunt, to the elections really gives five votes instead of one. . . ." As a friend to the ladies, the author assured his readers he had no wish to deprive women of their rights. But as their friend, he felt compelled to remind New Jersey's voting ladies that "female reserve and delicacy are incompatible with the duties of a free

226

elector." By 1807, New Jersey's government had disfranchised both women and free African Americans, and thus "the safety, quiet, good order and dignity of the state" was restored.[16]

What had happened to the keen interest in politics that had only a few years earlier prompted Eliza Wilkinson to note proudly that she and her friends had "commenced perfect statesmen"? Where were the women who had boldly announced their political actions in Edenton and other American cities and towns? Most were preoccupied with helping their husbands and fathers restore their farms and shops, or with re-establishing the much-desired rhythms of daily life for their children and themselves. In cities like Philadelphia, war widows were too busy attending to the needs of the boarders they had to take in to follow the news of politics and diplomacy. Free African American women, recently manumitted by masters or by state-mandated abolition of slavery, were too engaged in helping to create churches and other institutions for their own communities to follow the election rivalries among white men. Those African Americans who remained enslaved were caught up in daily struggles for survival that political leaders in the South condoned. Even in genteel society, few "perfect statesmen" could be found among the daughters and granddaughters of the Revolutionary War generation.

Had the war made little lasting impact on

women's role in American society? In the rush to a "return to normalcy" did American women and men embrace a social amnesia that allowed them to forget the Edenton Ladies, the Molly Pitchers, the Sybil Ludingtons, and the Eliza Wilkinsons? Would the changes that marked the great divide between colonial America and the new nation— the new acceptance of women's moral and intellectual abilities, the new emphasis on mothering rather than housewifery, the expectation of a companionate rather than an instrumental marriage—have occurred without the war for independence? Perhaps it would be well to remember that only seventy-two years after the Declaration of Independence—only a moment in the long flow of history—a group of women gathered at Seneca Falls to draft their own declaration. With it, a second war for independence was begun.

NOTES

Introduction: Clio's Daughters,
Lost and Found

1. For the quotations from Ellet, see the one-volume revised edition by Lincoln Diamant, ed., *Revolutionary Women in the War for American Independence: A One-Volume Revised Edition of Elizabeth Ellet's 1848 Landmark Series* (Westport, CT, and London: Praeger, 1998), pp. 143, 134.
2. For a recent study of women as historians, including Ellet, see Julie Des Jardins, *Women and the Historical Enterprise in America: Gender, Race, and the Politics of Memory, 1880–1945* (Chapel Hill: University of North Carolina Press, 2003).
3. See for example Mary Beth Norton, *Liberty's Daughters: The Revolutionary Experience of American Women, 1750–1800* (Ithaca, NY: Cornell University Press, 1980); Linda Kerber, *Women of the Republic: Intellect and Ideology in Revolutionary America* (Chapel Hill: University of North Carolina Press,

1980); Marylynn Salmon, *Women and the Law of Property in Early America* (Chapel Hill: University of North Carolina Press, 1989).

Chapter One: "The Easy Task of Obeying": Englishwomen's Place in Colonial Society

1. Quoted in Francis J. Bremer, *John Winthrop: America's Forgotten Founding Father* (New York: Oxford University Press, 2003), p. 321.
2. Cotton Mather, *Ornaments for the Daughters of Zion* (Boston, 1692); Benjamin Wadsworth, *The Well Ordered Family* (Boston, 1712); Samuel Chase, *Baron and Feme: A Treatise of the Common Law Concerning Husbands and Wives* (London, 1700); John Milton, *Paradise Lost* (New York: Penguin Classics, 2003).
3. William Blackstone, *Commentaries on the Laws of England* (London: Saunders and Benning, 1840). See Salmon, *Women and the Law of Property;* Norma Basch, *In the Eyes of the Law: Women, Marriage, and Property in Nineteenth-Century New York* (Ithaca, NY: Cornell University Press, 1982); Linda K. Kerber, *No Constitutional Right to Be Ladies: Women and the Obligations of Citizenship* (New York: Hill and Wang, 1998).
4. Norton, *Liberty's Daughters*; Laurel Ulrich, *Good Wives: Image and Reality in the Lives of Women in Northern New England, 1650–1750* (New York: Vintage, 1991).

5. George Francis Dow, ed., *The Holyoke Diaries* (Salem, MA: Essex Institute, 1919), pp. 48–81, quoted in Ulrich, *Good Wives,* p. 70.

6. Mary Cooper, Diary, December 14, 1769, New York Public Library.

7. Anne Randolph to St. George Tucker, September 23, 1788, "Randolph and Tucker Letters," *Virginia Magazine of History and Biography* 42, no. 1 (1934), pp. 49–50; Sally Hanschurst to Sally Forbes, 1762, in Sarah Hanschurst Papers, Library of Congress, Washington, D.C.; both printed in Sylvia R. Frey and Marion J. Morton, eds., *New Worlds, New Roles: A Documentary History of Women in Pre-Industrial America* (New York and Westport, CT: Greenwood Press, 1986), pp. 126–127.

8. Harriott Ravenel, *Eliza Pinckney* (New York: Scribners' Sons, 1896), pp. 115–116.

9. *Pennsylvania Chronicle,* August 10–17, 1767; Robert Barclay, *A Catechism and Confession of Faith* (Philadelphia, 1788), pp. 83–84; Anne Bradstreet, "To My Dear and Loving Husband," in *Works of Anne Bradstreet in Prose and Verse,* ed. John W. Ellis (Charleston, SC: A. E. Cutter, 1887), p. 394; Abigail Adams to John Adams, November 12–23, 1778, *The Book of Abigail and John: Selected Letters of the Adams Family, 1762–1784,* ed. L. H. Butterfield, Marc Friedlander, and Mary-Jo Kline (Cambridge, MA: Harvard University

Press, 1975), pp. 228–229; "The Jolly Orange Woman" (Worcester, MA, 1781). All of the above reprinted in Carol Berkin and Leslie Horowitz, eds., *Women's Voices / Womens' Lives: Documents in Early American History* (Boston: Northeastern University Press, 1998).

Chapter Two: "They say it is tea that caused it": Women Join the Protest Against English Policy

1. Susan Dion, "Women in the Boston Gazette, 1755–1775," *Historical Journal of Massachusetts* 14, no. 2 (June 1986), pp. 87–102.
2. Quoted in Arthur M. Schlesinger Sr., *The Colonial Merchants and the American Revolution, 1763–1776* (New York: Ungar Publishing Co., 1957), p. 107; *Boston Post-Boy,* November 16, 1767.
3. *Boston Evening Post,* February 12, 1770; see also Alfred Young, "The Women of Boston: 'Persons of Consequence' in the Making of the American Revolution, 1765–1776," in *Women and Politics in the Age of the Democratic Revolutions,* ed. Harriet Applewhite and Darlene Levy (Ann Arbor: University of Michigan Press, 1990), pp. 181–226.
4. For a discussion of Warren's role in the Revolution, see Rosemary Zagarri, A *Woman's Dilemma: Mercy Otis Warren and the*

American Revolution (Wheeling, IL: Harlan Davidson, 1995); Hannah Griffitts, "The Female Patriots," Edward Wanton Smith Collection, Haverford College Library, reprinted in *Milcah Martha Moore's Book*, ed. Catherine La Courreye Blecki and Karin A. Wulf (University Park: Pennsylvania State University Press, 1997), pp. 172–173.

5. *Boston News Letter*, quoted in Frank Moore, *Songs and Ballads of the American Revolution* (New York: New York Times and Arno Press, 1969), pp. 48–50.

6. Alice Morse Earle, ed., *Diary of Anna Green Winslow, A Boston School Girl of 1771* (Bedford, MA: Applewood Books, 1996), p. 32; Charity Clarke to [Joseph Jekyll], December 3, 1769, November 6, 1768, and June 16, [1769], Moore Family Papers, Columbia University.

7. Quoted in Louise Chipley Slavicek, *Women of the American Revolution* (Farmington Hills, MI: Lucent Books, 2003), p. 20.

8. See Laurel Ulrich, "Daughters of Liberty: Religious Women in Revolutionary New England," in *Women in the Age of the American Revolution*, ed. Ronald Hoffman and Peter Albert (Charlottesville: University of Virginia Press, 1989), pp. 211–243; Douglass Adair and John A. Schutz, eds., *Peter Oliver's Origin and Progress of the American Revolution: A Tory View* (San Marino, CA: The Huntington

Library, 1963), pp. 63–64; *Essex Gazette*, May 23, 1769; *Boston Evening Post*, quoted in Norton, *Liberty's Daughters*, p. 166.

9. William Tennent, "To the Ladies of South Carolina," *South Carolina Gazette*, August 2, 1774, reprinted in James H. Smylie, ed., "Presbyterians and the American Revolution: A Documentary Account," *Journal of Presbyterian History* 51 (1973), pp. 370–372.

10. The Resolves are reprinted in numerous texts. See, for example, Berkin and Horowitz, eds., *Women's Voices / Women's Lives*, pp. 180–181.

11. Arthur Iredell to James Iredell, January 31, 1775, printed in Don Higginbotham, ed., *The Papers of James Iredell*, vol. 1: 1776–1777 (Raleigh: North Carolina Division of Archives and History, 1976), pp. 282–284.

12. Quoted in Ray Raphael, *A People's History of the American Revolution: How the Common People Shaped the Fight for Independence* (New York: HarperCollins, 2002), p. 143; *Jemima Condict, Her Book* (Newark, NJ: Carteret Book Club, 1930), pp. 36–52.

13. *Rivington's Gazette*, March 9, 1775, quoted in Frank Moore and Peter Decker, eds., *The Diary of the American Revolution: From Newspapers and Original Documents* (Manchester, NH: Ayer Company Publishers, 1969), p. 10; quoted in Raphael, *A People's History*, p. 437; *Peter Oliver's Origins and*

Progress, pp. 97–98; Franklin B. Dexter, ed., *The Literary Diary of Ezra Stiles,* 3 vols. (New York: Charles Scribner's Sons, 1901), vol. 1, p. 480.

14. Esther Reed to Dennis DeBerdt, October 28, 1775, New-York Historical Society.

Chapter Three: "Thou can form no idea of the horrors": The Challenges of a Home-Front War

1. Mercy Otis Warren to John Adams, April 4, 1775, in Robert J. Taylor, ed., *The Adams Papers: The Papers of John Adams,* 3 vols. (Cambridge: Harvard University Press, 1977), vol. 1, pp. 413–14; Abigail Adams to John Adams, May 24, 1775, in L. H. Butterfield, Marc Friedlaender, and Mary-Jo Kline, eds., *The Book of Abigail and John: Selected Letters of the Adams Family, 1762–1784* (Boston: Northeastern University Press, 2002), pp. 84–86.

2. *A Narrative of the Excursion and Ravages of the King's Troops Under the Command of General Gage* (New York: New York Times and Arno Press, 1968), p. 20; Varnum Lansing Collins, ed., *A Brief Narrative of the Ravages of the British and Hessians at Princeton in 1776–1777* (New York: New York Times and Arno Press, 1968), pp. 36, 14.

3. Betsy Ambler to Mildred Smith, 1781, in "Cornwallis in Virginia," *Virginia Magazine of*

History and Biography 38 (1930), pp. 167–169; quoted in Richard Wheeler, *Voices of 1776: The Story of the American Revolution in the Words of Those Who Were There* (New York: Meridian Books, 1991), p. 287.

4. William Moultrie, *Memoir of the American Revolution* (New York: David Longworth, 1802), reprinted by Arno Press, 1969, vol. 1, p. 57; Linda K. Kerber, "'History Can Do It No Justice': Women and the Reinterpretation of the American Revolution," in Hoffman and Albert, eds., *Women in the Age of the American Revolution,* p. 10.

5. Moore, *Songs and Ballads,* p. 116, quoted in John C. Dann, "The Revolution Remembered—By the Ladies," *American Magazine* 3 (1987–1988), p. 73.

6. Quoted in Cynthia A. Kierner, *Southern Women in Revolution, 1776–1800: Personal and Political Narratives* (Columbia: University of South Carolina Press, 1998), p. 1.

7. Sara Josepha Hale, *Women's Record; or Sketches of Distinguished Women from Creation to A.D. 1854. Arranged in Four Eras with Selections from Female Writers of Every Age* (New York: Harper and Bros Publishers, 1855, reprinted by Source Book Press of New York, 1970), pp. 644–649; Diamant, ed., *Revolutionary Women,* p. 26; Kerber, "'History Can Do It No Justice,'" pp. 21–22.

8. Lucy Knox to Henry Knox, August 23, 1777, Gilder Lehrman Collection, Pierpont Morgan Library, New York City; Irwin Silber, ed., *Songs of Independence* (Harrisburg, PA: Stackpole Books, 1873), p. 87.

9. *Providence Gazette*, August 9, 1780, quoted in Elizabeth Cometti, "Women in the American Revolution," *New England Quarterly* 20, no. 3 (September 1947), pp. 320–346, at p. 337; Elizabeth Evans, *Weathering the Storm: Women of the American Revolution* (New York: Paragon House, 1989), p. 13.

10. *Independent Chronicle and Universal Advertiser* [Connecticut], October 9, 1777, in Raphael, *A People's History*, p. 150; Evans, *Weathering the Storm*, p. 13.

11. Ola Elizabeth Winslow, ed., *American Broadside Verse from Imprints of the Seventeenth and Eighteenth Centuries* (New Haven, CT: AMS Press, 1930), pp. 190–191. See also Joan R. Gundersen, *To Be Useful to the World: Women in Revolutionary America, 1740–1790* (New York: Twayne Publishers, 1996), p. 158; Cometti, "Women in the American Revolution," p. 330.

12. Quoted in Norton, *Liberty's Daughters*, p. 215; quoted in Slavicek, *Women of the American Revolution*, pp. 65–66. See also Cometti, "Women in the American Revolution," p. 333.

13. Norton, *Liberty's Daughters*, pp. 204–205; Kierner, *Southern Women in Revolution*, p. 18.

14. Abigail Adams to John Adams, March 16, 1776, in L. H. Butterfield, Marc Friedlaender, and Mary-Jo Kline, eds., *The Book of Abigail and John: Selected Letters of the Adams Family, 1762–1784* (Boston: Northeastern University Press, 1975), pp. 117–19; Jean Munn Bracken, ed., *Women in the American Revolution* (Carlisle, MA: Discovery Enterprises Ltd., 1997), p. 12; Collins, *A Narrative*, p. 15; Sylvia Frey, *Water from the Rock: Black Resistance in a Revolutionary Age* (Princeton, NJ: Princeton University Press, 1991), p. 117.

15. Quoted in Norton, *Liberty's Daughters*, pp. 205–206; Elaine Crane, ed., *The Diary of Elizabeth Drinker*, 3 vols. (Boston: Northeastern University Press, 1991), vol. 1, pp. 251, 266, 267, 271.

16. Bracken, *Women in the American Revolution*, p. 26.

17. Quoted in Norton, *Liberty's Daughters*, pp. 208–209.

18. Quoted in Kierner, *Southern Women in Revolution*, p. 18; Frey, *Water from the Rock*, p. 169; Evans, *Weathering the Storm*, pp. 16–17.

19. Norton, *Liberty's Daughters*, p. 199.

20. Evans, *Weathering the Storm*, p. 29; Gundersen, *To Be Useful to the World*, p. 156.

21. John C. Dann, ed., *The Revolution Remembered: Eyewitness Accounts of the War for Independence*

(Chicago: University of Chicago Press, 1980), pp. 130–131, 141, 187.

22. Phyllis R. Blakeley and John N. Grant, eds., *Eleven Exiles: Accounts of Loyalists of the American Revolution* (Toronto and Charlottetown, Canada: Dundurn Press, 1982), pp. 249–250; John H. Jackson, *Margaret Morris: Her Journal with Biographical Sketch and Notes* (Philadelphia: George W. McManus Company, 1949), p. 57.

23. Collins, *A Narrative,* pp. 14, 15; Moore and Decker, *The Diary of the American Revolution,* pp. 217, 378; Raphael, *A People's History,* p. 168.

24. Holly A. Mayer, *Belonging to the Army: Camp Followers and Community During the American Revolution* (Columbia: University of South Carolina Press, 1996), p. 59; Raphael, *A People's History,* p. 170.

25. Bracken, *Women in the American Revolution,* pp. 28, 16, quoted in Kerber, "'History Can Do It No Justice,'" p. 9.

26. Moore and Decker, eds., *The Diary of the American Revolution,* pp. 61–62; Raphael, *A People's History,* p. 149; Kierner, *Southern Women in Revolution,* p. 9.

27. Bracken, *Women in the American Revolution,* p. 12; Gundersen, *To Be Useful to the World,* p. 162; Dann, *The Revolution Remembered,* p. 11; Slavicek, *Women of the American*

Revolution (Farmington Hills, MI: Lucent Books, 2003), p. 32.

28. Esther DeBerdt Reed, *Sentiments of an American Woman* (Philadelphia: John Dunlap, 1780), Rare Book and Special Collections Division, Library of Congress.

29. [Esther DeBerdt Reed], *Ideas Relative to the Manner of Forwarding to the American Soldiers the Presents of the American Women* (Philadelphia: John Dunlap, 1780), Rare Book and Special Collections Division, Library of Congress.

30. Ibid.

31. "A Letter from a Lady in Philadephia to her Friend in this Place," June 20, 1780, *The Maryland Gazette,* July 21, 1780.

32. Marquis de Lafayette to Esther Reed, June 25, 1780, Papers of Joseph Reed, vol. 7, New-York Historical Society; Rosemary Fry Plakas, "American Women: A Library of Congress Guide for the Study of Women's History and Culture in the United States," Library of Congress, 2001; Lyman Butterfield, ed., *Letters of Benjamin Rush,* 2 vols. (Princeton: Princeton University Press, 1951), vol. 1, p. 253.

33. Anna Rawle to Mrs. Shoemaker, June 30, 1780, in "Letters and Diaries of Rebecca Shoemaker and Her Daughters Anna and Margaret Rawle," typescript, Am.

13745, Historical Society of Pennsylvania, Philadelphia.

34. Quoted in Norton, *Liberty's Daughters,* p. 184.
35. *Ideas Relative to the Manner*; George Washington to Esther Reed, August 10, 1780, Gratz Collection, Notable American Women, Case 7, Box 20, Historical Society of Pennsylvania, reprinted in John C. Fitzpatrick, ed., *The Writings of George Washington from the Original Manuscript Sources* (Washington, D.C.: United States Government Printing Office, 1937), pp. 350–351.
36. Sarah Bache to Benjamin Franklin, September 9, 1780, Yale University Library, published in *The Papers of Benjamin Franklin,* vol. 33 (New Haven, CT: Yale University Press, 1997), pp. 271–273.
37. *Pennsylvania Gazette,* September 27, 1780, Historical Society of Pennsylvania, Philadelphia.

Chapter Four: "Such a sordid set of creatures in human Figure": Women Who Followed the Army

1. Raphael, *A People's History,* p. 157.
2. John U. Rees, "'Some in rags and some in jags,' but none 'in velvet gowns': Insights on Clothing Worn by Female Followers of the

Armies During the American War for Independence," *Association of Living History, Farm and Agricultural Museums* 28, no. 4 (Winter 1990), p. 2.

3. Walter H. Blumenthal, *Women Camp Followers of the American Revolution* (Philadelphia: George S. MacManus Co., 1952), p. 22; Sylvia R. Frey, *The British Soldier in America: A Social History of Military Life in the Revolutionary Period* (Austin: University of Texas Press, 1981), pp. 20, 60; Linda G. DePauw, *Battle Cries and Lullabies: Women in War from Prehistory to the Present* (Norman: University of Oklahoma Press, 1998); John U. Rees, "'The Multitude of Women': An Examination of the Numbers of Female Camp Followers with the Continental Army," in *The Brigade Dispatch*, vol. 23, no. 4 (Autumn 1992), vol. 24, no. 1 (Winter 1993), and vol. 24, no. 2 (Spring 1993), reprinted in *Minerva: Quarterly Report on Women and the Military* 14, no. 2 (Summer 1996); Gundersen, *To Be Useful to the World*, p. 167.

4. Mayer, *Belonging to the Army*, p. 127; Raphael, *A People's History*, p. 157; James Kirby Martin, ed., *Ordinary Courage: The Revolutionary War Adventures of Joseph Plumb Martin* (St. James, NY: Brandywine Press, 1993), pp. 117–118.

5. Rees, "'Some in rags,'" p. 1; Slavicek, *Women of the American Revolution*, p. 50; John U.

Rees, "'The Proportion of Women which ought to be allowed...': An Overview of Continental Army Female Camp Followers," *The Continental Soldier* 8, no. 3 (Spring 1995), pp. 51–58, at p. 9.

6. Frey, *British Soldier in America*, p. 76; Rees, "'Proportion of Women,'" pp. 8–9.

7. Sally Smith Booth, *Women of '76* (New York: Hastings House, 1973), p. 183.

8. John U. Rees, "The Number of Rations Issued to the Women in Camp: New Material Concerning Female Followers with Continental Regiments," *The Brigade Dispatch*, vols. 27 and 28, p. 16; Booth, *Women of '76*, p. 183.

9. Rees, "'Proportion of Women,'" p. 5; Raphael, *A People's History*, p. 151; Charles K. Bolton, *The Private Soldier Under Washington* (Williamstown, MA: Corner House, 1976), p. 179.

10. Rees, "Multitude of Women," p. 5.

11. Frey, *British Soldier in America*, p. 20; Mayer, *Belonging to the Army*, p. 46; Rees, "Number of Rations," p. 3.

12. Blumenthal, *Women Camp Followers*, p. 63.

13. Raphael, *A People's History*, pp. 139–140.

14. Martin, *Ordinary Courage*, p. 80; Rees, "Multitude of Women," 1; Rees, "'Proportion of Women,'" p. 5; Booth, *Women of '76*, p. 174.

15. Gundersen, *To Be Useful to the World*, p. 164;

Mayer, *Belonging to the Army*, p. 144; *The Diary of the American Revolution*, compiled by Frank Moore and edited by John Anthony Scott (New York: Washington Square Press, 1969), pp. 368–369; Gundersen, *To Be Useful to the World*, p. 165; Slavicek, *Women of the American Revolution*, p. 37; Massachusetts Spy, June 27, 1782; Mayer, *Belonging to the Army*, p. 20.

16. Blumenthal, *Women Camp Followers*, p. 26; Mayer, *Belonging to the Army*, p. 51; Booth, *Women of '76*, pp. 34–35, 182; Slavicek, *Women of the American Revolution*, p. 48.

17. Booth, *Women of '76*, pp. 85, 86; DePauw, *Battle Cries and Lullabies*, pp. 121–122; Frey, *The British Soldier in America*, p. 62.

18. Rebecca D. Symmes, ed., *A Citizen-Soldier in the American Revolution: The Diary of Benjamin Gilbert in Massachusetts and New York* (Cooperstown: The New York State Historical Association, 1980), pp. 25, 30, 32.

19. DePauw, *Battle Cries and Lullabies*, p. 121; Raphael, *A People's History*, p. 155.

20. DePauw, *Battle Cries and Lullabies*, p. 121.

21. Lonnelle Aikman, "Patriots in Petticoats," *National Geographic* 49, no. 4 (October 1975), pp. 475–493, at p. 480.

22. Blumenthal, *Women Camp Followers*, p. 88; Aikman, "Patriots in Petticoats," p. 480.

23. Booth, *Women of '76*, pp. 103–104, 156–157; Hugh F. Rankin, ed., *Narratives of the*

American Revolution (Chicago: Lakeside Press, R. R. Donnelly & Sons Co., 1976), p. 307.

24. B. G. Moss, *Roster of the Loyalists in the Battle of Kings Mountain* (Blacksburg, SC: Scotia Hibernia, 1998), p. 64; Lyman C. Draper, *King's Mountain and Its Heroes: History of the Battle of King's Mountain, October 7, 1780, and the Events Which Led to It* (Johnson City, TN: The Overmountain Press, 1996), p. 292.

25. *Pennsylvania Packet*, December 11, 1781, quoted in Moore and Decker, *Diary of the American Revolution*, pp. 506–507.

Chapter Five: "How unhappy is war to domestic happiness": Generals' Wives and the War

1. Quoted in Joseph E. Fields, *Worthy Partner: The Papers of Martha Washington* (Westport, CT: Greenwood Press, 1994), p. xxi.

2. Martha Washington to Burwell Bassett, December 22, 1777, in Fields, *Worthy Partner*, p. 175.

3. George Washington to Martha Washington, June 18, 1776, in Fields, *Worthy Partner*, p. 160, and Martha Washington to Mercy Otis Warren, January 8, 1776, in Fields, *Worthy Partner*, p. 166.

4. George Washington to Martha Washington, June 18, 1775, in Fields, *Worthy Partner*, p. 160; Martha Washington to Mercy Otis

Warren, April 2, 1776, in Fields, *Worthy Partner,* p. 168.

5. Martha Washington to Elizabeth Ramsay, December 30, 1775, in Fields, *Worthy Partner,* pp. xxiii, 164.

6. Fields, *Worthy Partner,* pp. ix, xxiii, xxiv.

7. Martha Washington to Mercy Otis Warren, March 7, 1778, and Martha Washington to Anna Maria Bassett, August 28, 1776, in Fields, *Worthy Partner,* pp. 177–178, 172; Fields, *Worthy Partner.* p. xxiv.

8. Fields, *Worthy Partner,* p. 186; Marvin L. Brown Jr., *Baroness von Riedesel and the American Revolution: Journal and Correspondence of a Tour of Duty, 1776–1783* (Chapel Hill: University of North Carolina Press, 1965), p. 52n.

9. Lucy Knox to Henry Knox, August 23, 1777, Gilder Lehrman Collection, NYC.

10. Albert Cook Myers, ed., *Sally Wister's Journal, A True Narrative* (Philadelphia: Ferris & Leach, 1902); see also Richard M. Dorson, ed., *America Rebels: Narratives of the Patriots* (New York: Pantheon, 1953), pp. 219–236.

11. John F. Stegeman and Janet A. Stegeman, *Caty: A Biography of Catharine Littlefield Greene* (Athens: University of Georgia Press, 1977), p. 10.

12. Ibid., p. 21.

13. Ibid., p. 43.

14. Ibid., p. 49.
15. Ibid., pp. 80–81, 82.
16. Ibid., p. 92.
17. Ibid., p. 101.
18. William L. Stone, trans., *Letters and Journals Relating to the War of the American Revolution and the Capture of the German Troops at Saratoga by Mrs. General Riedesel* (Albany, NY: Joel Munsell, 1867), reprinted by the Arno Press (New York, 1968); Brown, *Baroness von Riedesel.*
19. Brown, *Baroness von Riedesel,* p. xxv.
20. Ibid., p. xxvii.
21. General Riedesel to Baroness von Riedesel, February 22, 1776, and Baroness von Riedesel to General Riedesel, March 3, 1776, in Brown, *Baroness von Riedesel,* pp. 148, 184–186.
22. General Riedesel to Baroness von Riedesel, March 26 and April 4, 1776, in Brown, *Baroness von Riedesel,* pp. 160–162, 166–167.
23. Baroness von Riedesel to her mother, May 3, 1776, in Brown, *Baroness von Riedesel,* pp. 186–187.
24. Stone, *Letters and Journals,* pp. 38, 40–41.
25. Ibid., pp. 47–48.
26. Ibid., pp. 68–70.
27. General Riedesel to Baroness von Riedesel, June 8, June 28, and September 23, 1776, in Stone, *Letters and Journals,* pp. 174–175, 176–178, 179–180.

28. Ibid., p. 113.
29. Ibid., pp. 114–115.
30. Ibid., pp. 119–120.
31. Ibid., pp. 125, 125n.
32. Ibid., pp. 127, 123.
33. Ibid., p. 128.
34. Ibid., p. 128n.
35. Ibid., p. 129.
36. Ibid., p. 135.
37. Ibid., p. 138.
38. Ibid., pp. 139, 142–144.
39. Ibid., pp. 144–145, 147.
40. Ibid., p. 164.
41. Thomas Jefferson to General Riedesel, May 3, 1780, quoted in Brown, *Baroness von Riedesel,* p. xxxiv.
42. Stone, *Letters and Journals,* pp. 180–181.
43. Ibid., pp. 184–185.

Chapter Six: "A journey a Crosse ye wilderness": Loyalist Women in Exile

1. Carol Berkin, *Jonathan Sewall: Odyssey of an American Loyalist* (New York: Columbia University Press, 1974), p. 106.
2. Raymond C. Werner, ed., "Diary of Grace Growden Galloway," *Pennsylvania Magazine of History and Biography,* vols. 55 (1931) and 58 (1934).
3. Hugh Edward Egerton, ed., *The Royal Commission on the Losses and Services of*

American Loyalists, 1783–1785 (New York: Arno Press and the New York Times, 1969), pp. 226, 311–312; North Callahan, *Flight from the Republic: The Tories of the American Revolution* (Indianapolis, IN: Bobbs-Merrill Company, 1967), pp. 47–48; Janice Potter-MacKinnon, *While the Women Only Wept: Loyalist Refugee Women in Eastern Ontario* (Montreal and Kingston, Canada: McGill-Queens University Press, 1993), pp. 56, 57.

4. Callahan, *Flight from the Republic*, pp. 47–48; James J. Talman, *Loyalist Narratives from Upper Canada* (New York: Greenwood Press, 1946), p. 318; Potter-MacKinnon, *While the Women Only Wept*, p. 63.

5. Callahan, *Flight from the Republic*, pp. 79–81.

6. July 9, 1777, William Livingston Papers, reel 5, p. 855, New Jersey Archives.

7. Potter-MacKinnon, *While the Women Only Wept*, p. 77.

8. Booth, *The Women of '76*, p. 66; Potter-MacKinnon, *While the Women Only Wept*, pp. 57, 48.

9. Potter-MacKinnon, *While the Women Only Wept*, p. 47; Sir Henry Clinton Papers, vol. 109, item 32, William L. Clements Library, University of Michigan.

10. Berkin, *Jonathan Sewall*, pp. 133–153; Callahan, *Flight from the Republic*, p. 91.

11. Mary Beacock Fryer, "Sara Sherwood: Wife and Mother, An 'Invisible Loyalist,'" in

Blakeley and Grant, eds., *Eleven Exiles*, pp. 245–261; Potter-MacKinnon, *While the Women Only Wept*, p. 92.

12. Potter-MacKinnon, *While the Women Only Wept*, p. 105.
13. "The Diary of Sarah Frost," in Walter Bates, *Kingston and the Loyalists of the "Spring Fleet" of 1783; with Reminiscences of early days in Connecticut; to which is appended a diary written by Sarah Frost on her Voyage to Saint John, New Brunswick, with the Loyalists of 1783* (n.p., n.d.), pp. 26–30; Callahan, *Flight from the Republic*, pp. 35, 42.
14. Callahan, *Flight from the Republic*, p. 86.
15. Peter Fisher, *The First History of New Brunswick* (Saint John's, New Brunswick: NonEntity Press, 1921), pp. 126–127.
16. Margaret Conrad, Toni Laidlaw, and Donna Smyth, eds., *No Place Like Home: Diaries and Letters of Nova Scotia Women, 1771–1938* (Halifax, Nova Scotia: Formac Publishing Company, 1988), p. 50; Rev. W. O. Raymond, *Winslow Papers*, A.D. 1776–1826 (Saint John's, New Brunswick: Sun Printing Company, 1901), pp. 150–152, 286–289.
17. Raymond, *Winslow Papers*, pp. 286–289; Carole Watterson Troxler, "Allegiance Without Community: East Florida as a Symbol of a Loyalist Contract in the South," in *Loyalists and Community in North America*, eds. Robert Calhoon, Timothy M. Barnes, and George A.

Rawlyk (Westport, CT: Greenwood Press, 1994), p. 127; Memorial of Cynthia Dwight, Public Record Office [Great Britain], Audit Office, class 13, vol. 80, folio 140.

Chapter Seven: "The women must hear our words": The Revolution in the Lives of Indian Women

1. See Richard White, *The Middle Ground: Indians, Empire, and Republics in the Great Lakes Region, 1650–1815* (Cambridge, England: Cambridge University Press, 1991).
2. See "The Sisters of Pocahontas: Native American Women in the Centuries of Colonization," in Carol Berkin, *First Generations: Women in Colonial America* (New York: Hill and Wang, 1996), pp. 52–78; see also James Axtell, *The Indian Peoples of Eastern America: A Documentary History of the Sexes* (New York: Oxford University Press, 1981); Theda Perdue, *Cherokee Women: Gender and Culture Change, 1700–1835* (Lincoln: University of Nebraska Press, 1998).
3. Neal Salisbury, ed., *Sovereignty and Goodness of God, Together with the Faithfulness of His Promises Displayed: Being a Narrative of the Captivity and Restoration of Mrs. Mary Rowlandson & Related Documents* (New York: Bedford/St. Martin's Press, 1997); James Everett Seaver, *A Narrative of the Life of Mrs.*

Mary Jemison (Canandaigua, NY: J. D. Bemis, 1824); see also K. Z. Derounian-Stodola and J. A. Levernier, *The Indian Captivity Narratives, 1550–1900* (New York: Twayne Publishers, 1993).

4. For biographies of Molly Brant, see Helen Caister Robinson, "Molly Brant: Mohawk Heroine," in Blakeley and Grant, eds., *Eleven Exiles,* pp. 117–141; James Taylor Carson, "Molly Brant: From Clan Mother to Loyalist Chief," in *Sifters: Native American Women's Lives,* ed. Theda Perdue (New York: Oxford University Press, 2001), pp. 48–60.

5. *Memoir of Lieutenant Colonel Tench Tilghman: Eyewitness Accounts of the American Revolution* (New York: New York Times and the Arno Press, 1971), p. 83; Carson, "Molly Brant," p. 54.

6. Quoted in Carson, "Molly Brant," p. 56; Blakeley and Grant, eds., *Eleven Exiles,* p. 125.

7. Quoted in Blakeley and Grant, eds., *Eleven Exiles,* p. 127.

8. For Nancy Ward, see Nancy Shoemaker, ed., *Negotiators of Change: Historical Perspectives on North American Indian Women* (New York: Routledge, 1994); Perdue, *Cherokee Women*; Norma Tucker, "Nancy Ward: Ghighau of the Cherokees," in *Georgia Historical Quarterly* 53 (June 1969), pp. 192–200; David Ray Smith, "Nancy Ward," in *Tennessee Encyclopedia of*

History and Culture, ed. Carroll Van West (Nashville, TN: Rutledge Hill Press, 1998), pp. 1033–1034.

9. Smith, "Nancy Ward," pp. 1033–1034.

10. For Queen Esther Montour, see Guy Abell, "Queen Esther—Indian Friend or Fiend?" *The Sunday Review*, Towanda, PA, August 20, 2000, p. 4A; Barbara Graymont, *The Iroquois in the American Revolution* (Syracuse, NY: Syracuse University Press, 1972); Mrs. George A. Perkins, *Early times on the Susquehanna* (Binghamton, NY: The Herald Company of Binghamton, 1906).

11. Seaver, *A Narrative of the Life of Mrs. Mary Jemison*, pp. 71–84.

12. For a discussion of domesticity in eighteenth-century white society, see "The Small Circle of Domestic Concerns," in Norton, *Liberty's Daughters*, pp. 3–39; for Seneca women, see Anthony Wallace, *Death and Rebirth of the Seneca* (New York: Vintage, 1972), pp. 239–340; "A Cherokee Women's Petition, May 2, 1817," in Berkin and Horowitz, eds., *Women's Voices/Women's Lives*, pp. 186–187.

Chapter Eight: "The day of jubilee is come": African American Women and the American Revolution

1. See Ira Berlin, *Generations of Captivity: A History of African-American Slaves* (Cambridge,

MA: Belknap Press of Harvard University Press, 2003), esp. table 1, "Slave Population of the American Colonies and the United States, 1680–1860."

2. Berlin, *Generations of Captivity*, p. 71.
3. For full discussions of the organization of slave labor, family life, and gender roles, see Berlin, *Generations of Captivity*; Philip Morgan, *Slave Counterpoint: Black Culture in the Eighteenth-Century Chesapeake and Lowcountry* (Chapel Hill: University of North Carolina Press, 1998); Frey, *Water from the Rock.*
4. "Lord Dunmore Promises Freedom to Slaves Who Fight for Britain, 1775," in *Principles and Acts of the Revolution in America,* ed. Hezekiah Niles (Baltimore: W. O. Niles, 1822), p. 375, reprinted in Richard D. Brown, *Major Problems in the Era of the American Revolution, 1760–1791: Documents and Essays* (Boston: Houghton Mifflin, 2000), pp. 259–260; Frey, *Water from the Rock,* p. 211.
5. *The Virginia Gazette,* November 5, 1775.
6. Raphael, *A People's History,* p. 98.
7. Benjamin Quarles, *The Negro in the American Revolution* (Chapel Hill: University of North Carolina Press, 1961), p. 25; Sylvia Frey, "Between Slavery and Freedom: Virginia Blacks in the American Revolution," *Journal of Southern History* 49 (1983), pp. 375–398;

Robert Selig, "The Revolution's Black Soldiers: They Fought for Both Sides in Their Quest for Freedom," *Journal of the Colonial Williamsburg Foundation* 19, no. 4 (Summer 1997), pp. 15–22.

8. Proclamation, June 30, 1779, British Headquarters (Sir Guy Carleton) Papers, PRO 30 / 55, quoted in part in Frey, *Water from the Rock,* pp. 113–114.

9. See Graham Russell Hodges, ed., *The Black Loyalist Directory: African Americans in Exile After the American Revolution* (New York: Garland Publishing, 1996), pp. 171–172.

10. Mary Louise Clifford, *From Slavery to Freetown: Black Loyalists After the American Revolution* (Jefferson, NC, and London: McFarland & Company, 1999), p. 50; Ellen Gibson Wilson, *The Loyal Blacks* (New York: G. P. Putnam's Sons, 1976), p. 95.

11. Henry Laurens to John Laurens, Charles Town, August 14, 1776, in David R. Chestnutt and Peggy J. Clark, eds., *Papers of Henry Laurens, January 5, 1776–November 1, 1777* (Chapel Hill: University of North Carolina Press, 1988), p. 233. See, for example, Frey, *Water from the Rock,* pp. 112–114, 117, 123–124.

12. Memoirs of the Life of Boston King, Houghton Library, Harvard University; Baroness Frederika Riedesel, *Letters and*

Journals (New York: New York Times and Arno Press, 1968), p. 188.

13. Frey, *Water from the Rock*, p. 193. *The Book of Negroes* was published as Graham Russell Hodges, ed., *The Black Loyalist Directory*, see note 9 above.

14. See Wilson, *The Loyal Blacks*, pp. 81–99, 100–116.

15. Ibid., 92–94; Clifford, *From Slavery to Freetown*, p. 55.

16. Wilson, *The Loyal Blacks*, p. 188; Frey, *Water from the Rock*, pp. 194–196; Clifford, *From Slavery to Freetown*, p. 111.

17. "On Being Brought from Africa to America" (1773), in William H. Robinson, *Phillis Wheatley in the Black American Beginnings* (Detroit: Broadside Press, 1975), p. 60.

18. Frey, *Water from the Rock*, p. 136.

19. "An Act for the Gradual Abolition of Slavery, 1780," reprinted in James T. Mitchell and Henry Flanders, compilers, *The Statutes at Large of Pennsylvania from 1682 to 1801*, vol. 10 (Harrisburg, PA, 1896–1915), pp. 67–73; Chief Justice William Cushing's opinion in *Walker v. Jennison*, 1781, quoted in Mary Wild, *Mumbet: The Life and Times of Elizabeth Freeman* (Greensboro, NC: Avisson Press, 1999), pp. 73–74.

20. Wild, *Mumbet*, p. 65.

21. Frey, *Water from the Rock*, pp. 208, 211–212.

22. Ibid., pp. 206–242; Edmund Randolph, quoted in Frey, *Water from the Rock*, p. 240.

Chapter Nine: "It was I who did it": Spies, Saboteurs, Couriers, and Other Heroines

1. See, for example, Elizabeth Ellet, *The Women of the American Revolution*, 3 vols., 4th ed. (New York: Haskell House Publishers, Ltd, 1969), and the modern abridged version, *Revolutionary Women in the War for American Independence: A One-Volume Revised Edition of Elizabeth Ellet's 1848 Landmark Series*, ed. Lincoln Diamant (Westport, CT: Praeger, 1998); Joseph J. Kelley Jr. and Sol Feinstone, *Courage and Candlelight: The Feminine Spirit of '76* (Harrisburg, PA: Stackpole Books, 1974); Evans, *Weathering the Storm*; Sally Smith Booth, *The Women of '76*; Melissa Lukeman Bohrer, *Glory, Passion, and Principle: The Story of Eight Remarkable Women at the Core of the Revolution* (New York: Atria Books, 2003); Alfred F. Young, *Masquerade: The Life and Times of Deborah Sampson, Continental Soldier* (New York: Alfred A. Knopf, 2004).
2. Booth, *Women of '76*, pp. 55–57; *Great Women in Connecticut History* (Permanent [Connecticut] Commission on the Status of Women, March 1, 1986); Raphael, *A People's History*, p. 157.
3. The Harriet Prudence Patterson Hall

Chapter of the National Society of the Daughters of the American Revolution of North Little Rock, Arkansas, provides this biographical information in its *Year Book, 2003–2004.*

4. Margaret Corbin's story was so well known that it was added to Ellet's biographical sketches by Diamant in his one-volume edition, pp. 112–113; it also appears in Evans, *Weathering the Storm,* pp. 10–11, and Booth, *Women of '76,* pp. 98–99.

5. V. T. Dacquino, *Sybil Ludington: The Call to Arms* (Fleishmanns, NY: Purple Mountain Press, 2000); Bohrer, *Glory, Passion, and Principle,* pp. 1–20.

6. A. H. Hoehling, *Women Who Spied* (New York: Dodd, Mead & Company, 1967), pp. 7–17; Diamant, ed., *Revolutionary Women,* pp. 113--115; Bohrer, *Glory, Passion, and Principle,* pp. 125–154; Booth, *Women of '76,* pp. 153–155; Elias Boudinot, *Journal of Events in the Revolution: Eyewitness Accounts of the American Revolution* (New York: The New York Times and Arno Press, 1968), pp. 50–51.

7. John Bakeless, *Turncoats, Traitors, and Heroes: Espionage in the American Revolution* (New York: Da Capo Press, 1998), pp. 252–265; Booth, *Women of '76,* pp. 243–244; see letter, undated, unsigned [Major Drummond] in Sir Henry Clinton Collection, the William Clements Library, University of Michigan;

Norman Polmar and Thomas B. Allen, *Spy Book: The Encyclopedia of Espionage* (New York: Random House Reference and Information Publishing, 1998), pp. 29, 50.

8. John H. McIntosh, *The Official History of Elbert County, Georgia, 1790–1935* (Atlanta, GA: Cherokee, 1968), pp. 221, 223; Beverly L. Pack, "Mammy Kate," *Historical Society of the Georgia National Guard* vol. 3, no. 3 (Spring/Summer 1993), pp. 10–12. Mammy Kate is a character in the first novel by former president Jimmy Carter, *The Hornet's Nest* (New York: Simon and Schuster, 2003).

9. Ellet, *Women of the American Revolution*, 1: 250–260; Dann, *The Revolution Remembered*, pp. 175–176.

10. Diamant, ed., *Revolutionary Women*, pp. 160–161.

11. Ellet, *Women of the American Revolution*, 3: pp. 149–152; Booth, *Women of '76*, pp. 256–257.

12. Diamant, ed., *Revolutionary Women*, p. 165; John A. Chapman, *School History of South Carolina* (Richmond, VA: Everett Waddey Company, 1897), pp. 134–137.

13. William Hintzen, "Betty Zane, Lydia Boggs, and Molly Scott: The Gunpowder Exploits at Fort Henry," *West Virginia History* 55 (1996), pp. 95–109.

Chapter Ten: "There is no Sex in soul":
The Legacy of Revolution

1. Frey, *Water from the Rock*, p. 206; Marylynn Salmon, *The Limits of Independence: American Women, 1760–1800* (New York: Oxford University Press, 1994), p. 83.

2. P. M. Zall, *Becoming American: Young People in the American Revolution* (Hamden, CT: Linnet Books, 1993), pp. 139, 173, 178.

3. For an interesting look at similar postwar discussions and outcomes regarding women's nature and role in society in other countries, see Carol Berkin and Clara Lovett, eds., *Women, War, and Revolution* (New York: Holmes Meier Publishers, 1980).

4. "To Eliza Norris—At Fairhill," reprinted in Berkin and Horowitz, eds., *Women's Voices / Women's Lives*, pp. 191–192.

5. Judith Sargent Murray to Miss Goldthwait, June 6, 1777, Judith Sargent Murray Papers, reel 1, vol. 1, Mississippi Department of History and Archives, reprinted in Berkin and Horowitz, eds., *Women's Voices / Women's Lives*, pp. 157–158.

6. Salmon, *The Limits of Independence*, pp. 81–82. For a biography and selected writings of Murray, see Sheila L. Skemp, *Judith Sargent Murray: A Brief Biography with Documents* (Boston and New York: Bedford Books, 1998).

7. Quoted in Berkin, *First Generations,* p. 201.

8. Berkin, *First Generations,* pp. 195–206; Norton, *Liberty's Daughters,* pp. 256–299; Ann D. Gordon, "The Young Ladies Academy of Philadelphia," in Carol Berkin and Mary Beth Norton, eds., *Women of America: A History* (Boston: Houghton Mifflin Company, 1979), pp. 68–91.

9. Quoted in Salmon, *The Limits of Independence,* p. 83.

10. "Philadelphia, 1787," reprinted in Berkin and Horowitz, eds., *Women's Voices / Women's Lives,* pp. 192–196.

11. Benjamin Rush, "Thoughts," in Berkin and Horowitz, eds., *Women's Voices / Women's Lives,* p. 194.

12. Susanna Haskell Rowson, "Women as They Are," in *Miscellaneous Poems* (Boston: Printed for the author by Gilbert & Dean & by W. P. & L. Blake, Corneill, 1804), reprinted in Berkin and Horowitz, eds., *Women's Voices / Women's Lives,* pp. 196–199.

13. Quoted in Berkin, *First Generations,* p. 198. For a full discussion of the *Gleaner* essays, see Skemp, *Judith Sargent Murray.*

14. Abigail Adams to John Adams, March 31, 1776; John Adams to Abigail Adams, April 14, 1776; Abigail Adams to John Adams, May 7, 1776, in Butterfield, Friedlander, and Kline, eds., *The Book of Abigail and John,* pp. 120–121, 121–123, 126–127.

15. For the suffrage clause in the New Jersey constitution of 1776, see Berkin and Horowitz, eds., *Women's Voices/Women's Lives,* p. 162; Newark *Centinel of Freedom,* 1797, the Newark Public Library, Newark, New Jersey; "A Friend to the Ladies," *Trenton True American,* October 18, 1802, reprinted in Berkin and Horowitz, eds., *Women's Voices/ Women's Lives,* pp. 184–185.

16. "A Supplement to the act entitled 'An act to regulate the election of members of the legislative council and general assembly, sheriffs and coroners in this state'; passed at Trenton the twenty-second day of February, one thousand seven-hundred and ninety-seven," in Acts of the 32nd General Assembly of New Jersey, Chapter 11, Section 1, 1807.

ACKNOWLEDGMENTS

Where to begin? This book has been swirling around in my head for three decades. Its themes and cast of characters have appeared in countless lectures in the classroom and in public talks I have given across the country to women's clubs, Revolutionary War organizations, and historical society members. I have regaled family and friends—and occasionally strangers—with tales of camp followers, spies and generals' wives at dinner parties and Thanksgiving feasts, much to the embarrassment of my children. Over the years, I have come to feel that the women who appear in this book are intimate friends, long-standing friends, for I have read their diaries and letters and accounts of their deeds, and I have relived—with them and for them—the years of crisis that led to American independence.

Along the way, a number of people have helped me turn my stories into a coherent book. Scholars like Mary Beth Norton and Linda Kerber, Marylynn Salmon and Elaine Crane wrote the books that established early American women's history as a legitimate and important field.

Without their work, this book would not have been possible. Over the long months of writing and revising, I had the good fortune to work once again with a group of historians who gather twice a month at my dining room table to nibble at croissants and cakes, drink strong coffee, and critique one another's work. We call ourselves the Salon, a harmless affectation that we indulge. These remarkable colleagues and friends—Angelo Angelis, Kathleen Feeley, Cindy Lobel, Philip Papas, and Iris Towers—read and reread drafts of every chapter until they were satisfied I had done my best. My colleague at the City University Graduate Center, Thomas Kessner, also read endless drafts, offered astute observations, and added just the right amount of encouragement with every stinging critique. My thanks also to friends who answered frantic SOS pleas for sources: Professors Betty Wood, Sylvia Frey, Mary Beth Norton, Mary-Jo Kline, Catherine Clinton, Patricia Brady, and Elaine Crane.

My agent, Dan Green, did far more than the matchmaking between author and editor that is an agent's first duty. He too read the manuscript in all its versions. I knew when my phone rang early in the morning that it was Dan, ready to deliver his comments and suggestions. My editor, the extraordinary Jane Garrett, watched over me throughout the months of writing. She sent encouragement and provided guidance on a regular basis.

Michael Graziosi, a promising young historian, did much of the scavenging for articles and primary documents, spending time in the bowels of the New York Public Library, carrying a book bag full of obscure tomes, and feeding dimes into a variety of copy machines at local archives. Greg Toft, my undergraduate research assistant, did library duty and listened to my tales of woe about books that were not on the proper library shelf. Jessica Gonzales, the administrative assistant to the Department of History at Baruch College, demonstrated her professionalism by never tiring of reminding me what the access code was to the duplicating machine. My thanks also to the talented and able women at Knopf: Emily Owens, who guided the manuscript through production, and Susannah Sturgis, who eliminated random commas, corrected spelling, and made the prose more readable wherever these changes were badly needed.

As always, I give thanks to my children, Hannah and Matthew. They are the reason living in the present brings as much joy to me as studying the past. Finally, this book is dedicated to my brother, Mark, and my sister, Sylvia. I hope I have made them proud.